Evolutionary Economics and Social Complexity Science

Volume 8

The Japanese Association for Evolutionary Economics (JAFEE) always has adhered to its original aim of taking an explicit "integrated" approach. This path has been followed steadfastly since the Association's establishment in 1997 and, as well, since the inauguration of our international journal in 2004. We have deployed an agenda encompassing a contemporary array of subjects including but not limited to: foundations of institutional and evolutionary economics, criticism of mainstream views in the social sciences, knowledge and learning in socio-economic life, development and innovation of technologies, transformation of industrial organizations and economic systems, experimental studies in economics, agent-based modeling of socio-economic systems, evolution of the governance structure of firms and other organizations, comparison of dynamically changing institutions of the world, and policy proposals in the transformational process of economic life. In short, our starting point is an "integrative science" of evolutionary and institutional views. Furthermore, we always endeavor to stay abreast of newly established methods such as agent-based modeling, socio/econo-physics, and network analysis as part of our integrative links.

More fundamentally, "evolution" in social science is interpreted as an essential key word, i.e., an integrative and /or communicative link to understand and re-domain various preceding dichotomies in the sciences: ontological or epistemological, subjective or objective, homogeneous or heterogeneous, natural or artificial, selfish or altruistic, individualistic or collective, rational or irrational, axiomatic or psychological-based, causal nexus or cyclic networked, optimal or adaptive, micro- or macroscopic, deterministic or stochastic, historical or theoretical, mathematical or computational, experimental or empirical, agent-based or socio/econo-physical, institutional or evolutionary, regional or global, and so on. The conventional meanings adhering to various traditional dichotomies may be more or less obsolete, to be replaced with more current ones vis-á-vis contemporary academic trends. Thus we are strongly encouraged to integrate some of the conventional dichotomies.

These attempts are not limited to the field of economic sciences, including management sciences, but also include social science in general. In that way, understanding the social profiles of complex science may then be within our reach. In the meantime, contemporary society appears to be evolving into a newly emerging phase, chiefly characterized by an information and communication technology (ICT) mode of production and a service network system replacing the earlier established factory system with a new one that is suited to actual observations. In the face of these changes we are urgently compelled to explore a set of new properties for a new socio/economic system by implementing new ideas. We thus are keen to look for "integrated principles" common to the above-mentioned dichotomies throughout our serial compilation of publications. We are also encouraged to create a new, broader spectrum for establishing a specific method positively integrated in our own original way.

More information about this series at http://www.springer.com/series/11930

Kazuhiro Okuma

The Evolving Relationship between Economy and Environment

Theory and the Japanese Experience

Springer

Kazuhiro Okuma
Tohoku University
Sendai, Miyagi, Japan

ISSN 2198-4204 ISSN 2198-4212 (electronic)
Evolutionary Economics and Social Complexity Science
ISBN 978-981-13-5048-1 ISBN 978-981-10-4100-6 (eBook)
DOI 10.1007/978-981-10-4100-6

Printed on acid-free paper

This Springer imprint is published by Springer Nature
The registered company is Springer Nature Singapore Pte Ltd.
The registered company address is: 152 Beach Road, #21-01/04 Gateway East, Singapore 189721, Singapore

Preface

Many activities in the world, whether in practice or in research, tend to be pursued exclusively within their fields, thereby generating gaps between issues that are in fact intrinsically interlinked. These gaps prevent us from making sense of the whole reality and taking appropriate steps. It is often more crucial to bridge these gaps than it is to advance in one's own field. This applies to the deeply interconnected issues of economics and environmental policy. This book aims to help bridge the gap between them.

This study has taken shape over a decade of my research, though it is also supported by my longer experience in policy development as a bureaucrat. This experience has impressed upon me the need to bridge the gap between policy reality and economic thought. This need has been particularly driven home, for example, when seeing politicians' discontent with the inadequate explanation of possible Green Growth that is provided by orthodox economics, as well as when facing stiff opposition from businesses regarding scientifically desirable policies. Thus, by applying economic thought with a focus on the policy aspect as its theoretical basis, and by using hands-on information on policy process as empirical data, this study tries to make sense of the reality of economy and the environment.

Some of the arguments in this book have previously appeared as articles. The main elements of Part II were published in *Evolutionary and Institutional Economics Review* in 2012, while the essence of Part III appeared as an article in the same journal in 2016. The overall story has also appeared in a book titled *Is Green Growth Possible?* in Japanese, which was published by Fujiwara-shoten in 2015. The present book has been substantially revised since then; the information has been updated and various important ideas have been added.

The studies described in this book intend to advance an evolutionary and institutional economic approach to the issues of environment and sustainability. This approach has great potential to generate fruitful knowledge, and a wide field of research lies before us. It is my sincere hope that this work will serve as a contribution to the development of research in this field.

This book owes much to many colleagues and friends. I would particularly like to thank Hiroyasu Uemura of the Yokohama National University, who has continuously provided valuable advice from the beginning of my academic research to its publication. My appreciation also goes to Yuji Aruka, editor-in-chief of *Evolutionary Economics and Social Complexity Science*, for making this publication possible. I am deeply grateful to Robert Boyer for his precious advice over the course of my research, which greatly encouraged me. I wish to thank the scholars of the *régulation* school, particularly Toshio Yamada, Hiroyuki Uni, and Hiroshi Nishi, for their valuable advice and warm encouragement. I am grateful to Eiji Hosoda and Fumikazu Yoshida, who provided me with valuable comments from the viewpoint of environmental economics and policy studies. I am indebted to Yoshinori Shiozawa for providing insights into evolutionary economics. A part of the studies in this book was supported by Japan Society for the Promotion of Science (JSPS) KAKENHI Grant Number JP16K12656. Last but not least, my deepest appreciation goes to my wife Harumi, for her constant support and warm encouragement.

Sendai, Japan
January 2017

Kazuhiro Okuma

Contents

Part IV Conclusion

Part I
Overview

Chapter 1
Introduction

1.1 Understanding the Evolving Relationship Between Economy and the Environment

Humankind's economic activities have been rapidly growing ever since the Industrial Revolution. The limits of the earth's resources have long since been recognized and the crisis of sustainability clearly pointed out. Climate change is now manifesting itself, causing severe natural disasters, while the drive for economic growth is intensifying under global capitalism. Can we avoid a catastrophe of the environment? Can the economy continue to grow? What will happen in our future?

Though the relationship between economy and the environment has been studied and discussed in various ways, we are still looking for the answer to these questions. This book seeks a new perspective on this issue by exploring a unique approach based on evolutionary and institutional economics, as well as by analyzing the issue both theoretically and empirically.

Behind this approach is a belief that the relationship between economy and the environment cannot be adequately understood through the logic of either one of them: their interaction needs to be understood as a coevolving process.

1.1.1 Beyond Divided Thoughts on Economic Growth and Environmental Measures

Abnormal weather has now become a normal event. Record-breaking high temperatures and unprecedentedly strong hurricanes and typhoons frequently hit us. The degradation of forests and biodiversity are not curbed. Scientists are issuing increasingly strong warnings of the crisis taking place in the earth's ecosystem. It

K. Okuma, *The Evolving Relationship between Economy and Environment*,
Evolutionary Economics and Social Complexity Science 8,
DOI 10.1007/978-981-10-4100-6_1

is already painfully clear that the current economic activities are not sustainable. Anxiety about our future is permeating the air like dark clouds in front of us.

On the other hand, the world's central concern continues to be economic growth. Money instantaneously moves around the world in search of profits. Businesses and politicians alike react nervously to a slight change in growth rate and stock prices. Even political news, such as elections or diplomacy, is reported in the context of how it impacts the markets.

These are both realities that we are facing. They can seem contradictory to each other, although in most cases they exist independently without their relationship even being considered. Facing these two realities, how should we understand the world and look toward the future?

One may see the world from either of these two viewpoints. For example, one may continue pursuing unchecked economic growth, under the belief that environmental problems will be resolved when innovative technologies are someday invented. Or one may argue, instead, for desirable measures and technologies to contain economic activities within the earth's capacity, based on the recognition that the earth's ecosystem is the basis of all human activities. In fact, most arguments we see on economy and the environment belong to one of these two approaches.

However, regarding the former and observing how history shows that economic growth and technological progress have been causing degradation of the global environment, can we believe in the argument that this time they will solve the problem? Regarding the latter, even if ideal policies are designed by putting aside the reality that economic growth is so strongly pursued, the feasibility of such policies must be questioned.

When searching for a future that is based on reality rather than on dreamy ideas, we can hardly find a satisfactory guide in either of these two ways of thinking. If we are to sincerely seek a vision for the future, we need to look squarely at both realities—at both the "crisis of the earth's ecosystem" and the "pursuit of economic growth"—without closing our eyes to one of them, and thus fundamentally review the relationship between economy and the environment.

After the world economic crisis in 2008, the idea of "Green Growth" emerged and was advocated by many countries and international organizations. Is Green Growth possible? Theoretically clarifying its possibility and limits would be one key to answer this question.

1.1.2 Approach from Evolutionary and Institutional Economics

In order to make sense of the world, theory is required. The world is too complex to understand by intuition. If one is to understand it for oneself, without being caught up in prejudices or existing discourses, one needs to get a good look at its cross-section with the aid of some theories and concepts.

Behind the discourses we hear on economy and the environment, theories exist. Whether explicitly or implicitly, these theories significantly influence the framing of our thoughts. Behind the discourse emphasizing economic growth lies economics. It presumes that the market mechanism enables an efficient allocation of resources and regards the environment as one of the elements to be traded therein. To put it another way, this point of view believes that the economy contains the environment, and that the economy is located in a superior position. Behind the discourse highlighting the finite nature of the earth, on the other hand, lie the environmental sciences. They see the earth as a physical, thermodynamic, or ecological system and recognize the economy as one of its components. In this point of view, the situation is reversed: the environment is believed to contain the economy and to be located in a superior position. It is difficult for these two discourses to meet on the same plane, since their ways of seeing the world are different.

Environmental economics, in its wider meaning of "economics related to environmental problems," is in a position to generate recognition that takes into consideration both economic and environmental principles. However, when it is bound by a theoretical premise of optimal equilibrium by market mechanisms, the field may deal with the environment under economic principles, rather than taking both equally into account.

To consider the relationship between economy and the environment from a new perspective, we need to start by reconsidering theories to rely on. We perceive economy and the environment as two systems that exist in parallel, interact with each other, and thus change. That is, we see them as coevolving systems. As a theoretical basis for this, we will explore, in this book, an approach from the angle of evolutionary and institutional economics. Its viewpoints, which emphasize coordination by institutions and changes over time, enable us to relativize economy as a system that changes through its interactions with nature and society.

1.1.3 Theoretical Framework and Empirical Analysis

There are various trends in evolutionary and institutional economics, among which this book relies mainly on *régulation* theory and post-Keynesian theory (in particular, the Kaleckian model). These theories are compatible, both having been developed with special attention to macroeconomic issues. The strength of the former lies in its historical analysis of institutional coordination and economic growth, while that of the latter lies in its mathematical modeling of growth with a focus on social relation. By combining them in complementary manner, and by referring to a wider range of related concepts as needed, we build a theoretical framework to analyze economy and the environment. To build a robust basis for this framework, this book starts with the insights of Karl Polanyi. The reason and meanings of this approach will be further explained in Sect. 2.2.

The aim of this book is to make sense of the real issues in front of us. For this purpose, this book conducts an empirical analysis based on the framework above. Economy and the environment have evolved by interacting with each other, throughout history. We will review this historical transformation from a new perspective. Japan—having experienced high economic growth, severe pollution, and intensive countermeasures—provides one of the best cases to empirically analyze the relationship between economy and the environment and, in particular, the possibilities and limits of Green Growth. This book focuses on the relationship between economy and the environment in Japan, from the postwar era to today. When and how were environmental measures strengthened in response to economic growth? Have environmental measures ever impacted economic growth? How? We will try to answer these questions using not only qualitative information, but also quantitative indices and an econometric analysis. This will be the basis from which to explore visions of the future.

Thus, by conducting combined theoretical and empirical analyses, this book searches for a deeper and more realistic perception of the relationship between economy and the environment.

The results gained from these analyses will include a clear understanding of the mechanisms to develop environmental institutions and the factors currently impeding them. The historical trend of the economy to grow by consuming nature will also be highlighted. We will face the difficulties of institutional coordination of the economy. On the other hand, the possibility of Green Growth, where environmental measures contribute to economic growth, will also be explored.

Let us look into the future, based on these historical recognitions. What we see may not be a rosy picture that one can paint on a blank canvas. However, this will be the road that leads to a vision with true hope.

1.2 Plan of the Book

This book is organized as follows. After this introduction, Chap. 2 provides further explanations on the aim and approach of this book, in order to share a basic recognition of the issues before entering into detailed analysis. Section 2.1 gives an overview of world history, in terms of economy and the environment, and indicates the viewpoints and issues to be explored in the book. Section 2.2 explains the book's theoretical approach, so as to clarify our place amidst the various economic theories.

From this basis, Part II conducts a theoretical analysis of the relationship between economy and the environment, and Part III carries out an empirical analysis of the Japanese experiences. The relationships between chapters are shown as a diagram in Fig. 1.1.

In the theoretical analysis in Part II, Chap. 3 considers a recognition of the socioeconomic system as the basis of the framework, introducing the concept of triple reproductions of economy, environment, and society. It also discusses a way

Fig. 1.1 Structure of chapters

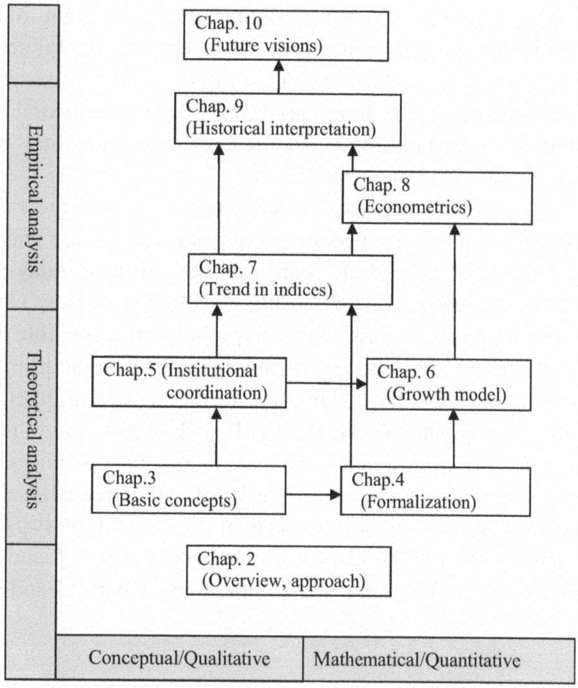

to capture environmental measures as costs. Chapter 4 formalizes these concepts, exploring a way to mathematically present the relationship of triple reproductions and the cost of environmental measures.

Based on the concept of the socioeconomic system above, Chap. 5 discusses the institutional coordination of the relationship between economy and the environment (hereafter called the "economy-environment nexus"), mainly based on *ré gulation* theory. Section 5.1 elaborates on the dynamics of institutional coordination, using some key concepts such as the structure of actors and feedback and indicating a unique nature of the economy-environment nexus, in which spatial or temporal gaps between economy, environment, and society cause delayed coordination. Section 5.2 considers the process of transformation, referring to concepts of crisis and institutional change. Section 5.3 analyzes the relationship between the economy-environment nexus and the growth regime. The impacts of environmental measures on the growth regime are identified by focusing on the effects of environmental costs.

Chapter 6 develops a variant of Kaleckian model that incorporates environmental costs in order to formally analyze their impacts on the growth regime, and thus analyzes the possibility of Green Growth and its conditions.

Part III conducts an empirical analysis of Japanese history since the postwar era, using the framework developed in Part II. Chapter 7 gives an overview of the transformation of the economy-environment nexus by tracing its history in three aspects: economy (in particular, growth), environment (in particular, environmental burdens), and society (in particular, the formulation of institutions); as well as by conducting a long-term estimation of environmental costs.

Chapter 8 conducts an econometric analysis, based on the Kaleckian model developed in Chap. 6 and applying the environmental costs estimated in Chap. 7. It thus quantitatively evaluates how environmental measures have historically impacted economic growth.

By synthesizing these results, Chap. 9 interprets in detail how institutional coordination of the economy-environment nexus, and its relation to the growth regime, has changed in Japan from the 1960s to today.

Finally, based on the results of these analyses, Chap. 10 (Part IV) explores visions into the future, with a hypothesis of a possible evolutionary process.

As noted, the chapters of this book, which range from theoretical to empirical and from conceptual/qualitative to mathematical/quantitative, interlink with each other, composing a system (Fig. 1.1). The best way to read the book is from start to finish. However, readers can also take up specific chapters according to their interests, though it is still suggested that they read closely related chapters together. For example, readers interested in conceptual analysis may read Chaps. 3 and 5; those interested in historical analysis, Chaps. 7 and 9; those in mathematical modeling (and its empirical application), Chaps. 4 and 6 (and Chaps. 7 and 8).

Chapter 2
Evolutionary and Institutional Approach to Economy and the Environment

To gain insight into the future, we need to understand the present. To understand the present, we need to understand the past. This book analyzes the relationship between economy and the environment from a historical perspective. As a prologue to this book, let us overview the long-term history of the relationship between economy and the environment in the world, so that we share an understanding of the book's aim and of the issues.

In addition, we will add some explanations of our theoretical approach in Sect. 2.2.

2.1 Economy and the Environment in World History

2.1.1 World Economic Growth and Environmental Burdens

The economic activities of humankind have grown rapidly since the industrial revolution and the emergence of the capitalist economy. According to the estimation by Maddison (2001, 2008), growth of the world's GDP gained speed around 1820 and further accelerated around 1950, after the Second World War (Fig. 2.1).

How, then, have environmental burdens changed? Carbon dioxide emission is one indicator for which long-term data is available. According to the estimation by the Oak Ridge Laboratory (Borden et al. 2016), it has been continuously increasing since around 1820, having accelerated around 1950 (Fig. 2.2).

The long-term view shows that the scale of the economy and environmental burdens have been increasing in tandem, demonstrating the close relationship between them. As a result, environmental burdens have obviously exceeded the carrying capacity of the earth. The latest scientific knowledge tells us that global

K. Okuma, *The Evolving Relationship between Economy and Environment*,
Evolutionary Economics and Social Complexity Science 8,
DOI 10.1007/978-981-10-4100-6_2

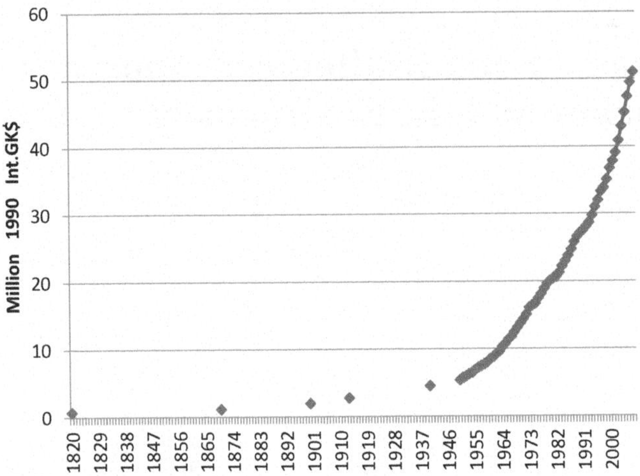

Fig. 2.1 Long-term trend of world GDP

GHG (greenhouse gas) emissions need to be reduced by 40–70% by 2050 and taken to near zero or below by 2100 (IPCC 2014).[1] This means that CO_2 emissions need to be sharply reduced toward two orbit zones in 2050 and 2100, as shown in Fig. 2.2.

In view of the past increasing trend and its correlation with GDP, we cannot help asking questions as to whether CO_2 emission can be reduced and, if so, whether GDP can continue to increase. The idea of "de-coupling" this correlation has emerged, though this may end up as a case of idealism if it lacks mechanisms to enable it in real world.

So far, both the economy and the environmental burdens have been growing at accelerated rates. What has generated this trend of growth? First, we must understand the driving forces behind it. Then, if there have been periods when the correlation between the two has weakened, we need to understand how that was realized. This can form a basis to consider whether and how environmental burdens can be reduced from now on.

[1]The fifth assessment report of the IPCC (Intergovernmental Panel on Climate Change) considered multiple scenarios on long-term mitigation pathways. Among these were "mitigation scenarios in which it is likely that the temperature change caused by anthropogenic GHG emissions can be kept to less than 2 °C relative to pre-industrial levels." These scenarios are characterized by atmospheric concentrations in 2100 of about 450 ppm CO_2eq, which requires significantly lower levels of emissions, as described here (IPCC 2014).

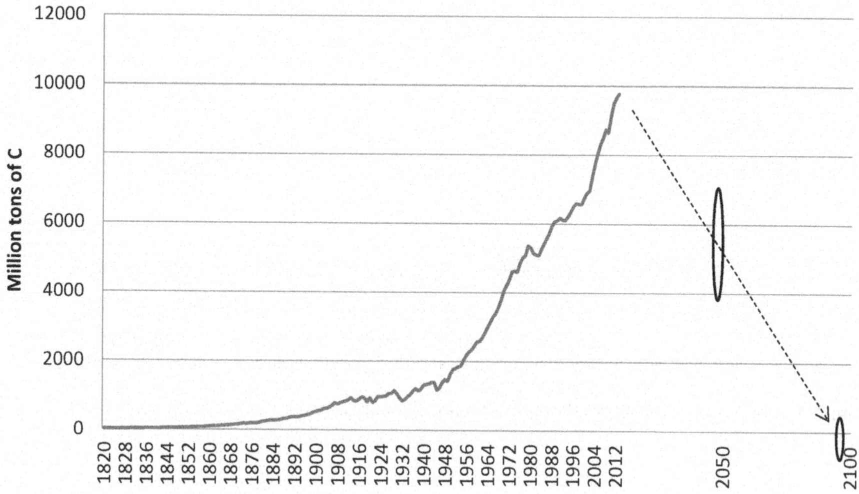

Fig. 2.2 Long-term trend of world CO_2 emission

2.1.2 Economic Growth and Its Factors in Regions and Periods

In order to step forward in the above direction, let us look at economic growth and its factors by dividing regions and periods. The mechanisms of economic growth are not uniform, but are both temporally and spatially diverse. So is the environmental burden. By observing regional and periodical characteristics, we can better understand the mechanisms of both the growing economy and the growing environmental burden.

Here, we look at developed countries where data is available. Maddison (2001) estimated average growth rates by regions and by periods divided at 1820, 1870, 1913, 1950, and 1973, when the trend apparently changed.[2] His data can be presented as Fig. 2.3. It should be noted that the numbers in Fig. 2.3 and the following are growth rates, while those in Figs. 2.1 and 2.2, above, are absolute values. Absolute values continue exponentially increasing, as long as growth rates are positive, even if low.

As typically seen in Western Europe, where a capitalist economy was first established, a relatively high growth rate continued from the economy's take-off until the end of the nineteenth century. It then fell in the first half of the twentieth century. After the Second World War, significantly rapid growth was realized from 1950 to 1973, but slowed down after the 1970s. It is said that there were two periods

[2]We present data up to 1998, referring to Maddison (2001), though there are more recent estimations by Maddison (2003) and other studies done by his group. This is because data on labor productivity is not shown in the latter.

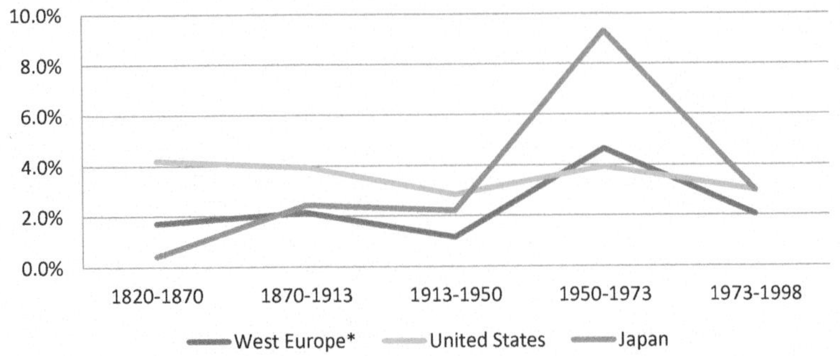

* Austria, Belgium, Denmark, Finland, France, Germany, Italy, Netherland, Norway, Sweden, Switzerland and United Kingdom; the same applies hereafter.

Fig. 2.3 Long-term change in GDP growth rate (Annual average compound growth rate)

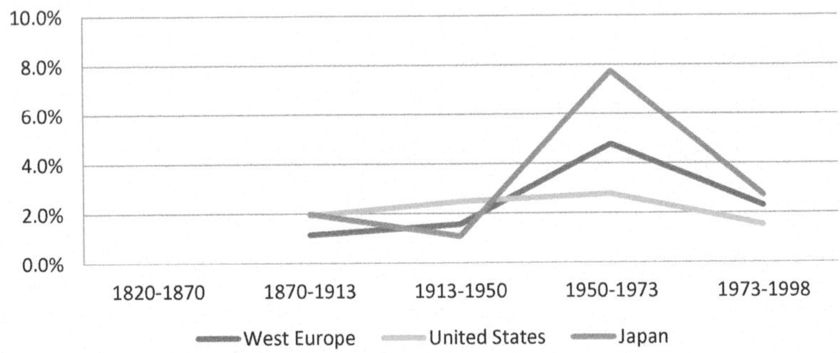

Fig. 2.4 Long-term change in growth rate of labor productivity (Annual average compound growth rate)

of growth, that is, the late nineteenth century and the postwar era in the twentieth century.

When analyzing factors of growth, we usually look first at labor productivity. Based on the estimation by Maddison (2001), growth rates in labor productivity can be calculated and presented as Fig. 2.4. High growth rates from 1950 to 1973 are significant. On the other hand, growth rates were low in the period until 1913. This shows that the growth in the nineteenth century involved mainly a quantitative increase in labor input, while the growth in the postwar era was based on a qualitative improvement of labor productivity.

As was just described, the mode of economic growth is not uniform but changes over time. Behind this are changes in institutions that support the economy. *Ré gulation* theory explains the historical transformation of economic growth with a focus on institutional coordination, as follows.

In the nineteenth-century, the growth was realized by subsuming additional labor forces and markets from outside, under institutional characteristics such as low wages and free competition. This is called extensive accumulation. On the other hand, the high growth in the postwar era was generated by a positive growth cycle between labor productivity and consumer demand, which was realized by a labor–management compromise, including high wages, under the welfare states' institutions. This growth regime is called intensive accumulation (Boyer 1986).

Though these analyses of the characteristics of each period are quite helpful in understanding the mechanism of economic growth, they have not explained what kind of role the environment plays there. This is the issue that we must address. We have estimated the growth rate in carbon productivity (GDP per unit CO_2 emission) for the periods by Maddison, using the data of Oak Ridge Laboratory (Borden et al. 2016), which is shown in Fig. 2.5. It should be noted that we refer to carbon productivity here, due to data availability, although resource productivity or environmental productivity should ideally be obtained by taking into account all kinds of environmental burdens.

In the early stage of the capitalist economy, carbon productivity decreased. This appears to reflect the shift from an economy relying on the material circulation of nature (e.g., agriculture) to one relying on fossil fuels and thus subsuming additional environment and resources. After that, carbon productivity began to increase in the first half of the twentieth century. However, it lost speed in the high-growth era from 1950 to 1973, and even turned to a decrease in Japan. This shows a clear contrast with labor productivity, which rapidly increased in this period. The high growth in this period was supported by an expanding consumption of the environment.

On the other hand, after the 1970s, carbon productivity increased to some extent, particularly in Japan. Other pollutants were also reduced by government regulations

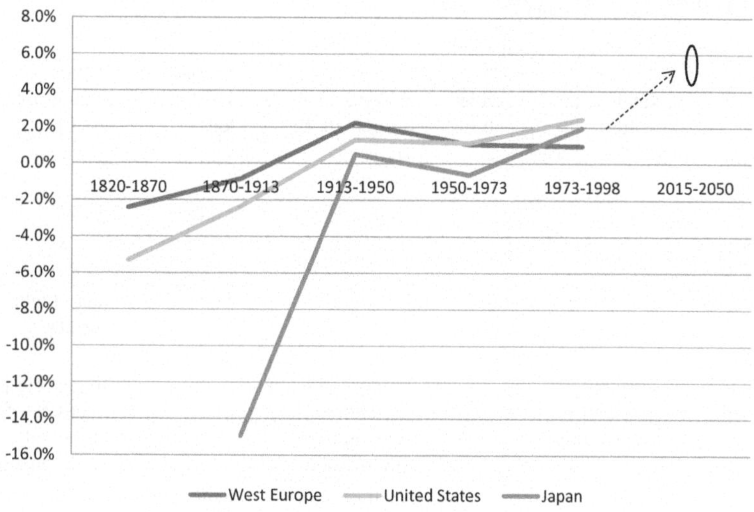

Fig. 2.5 Long-term change in growth rate of carbon productivity (Annual average compound growth rate)

in the 1970s, meaning that wider environmental productivity should have increased then.

Here, let us think about the future. As described in Fig. 2.2, worldwide CO_2 emissions need to be reduced by 40–70% in 2050, which requires larger reductions in developed countries. So far, it was agreed (at a past G8 summit meeting) that developed countries should aim at reductions of more than 80%. For this to happen, carbon productivity needs to rise at a significantly higher rate than that of economic growth. A simple calculation shows that carbon productivity needs to increase at around 5% per annum, even when economic growth is at 0%. It needs to be at around 6% when economic growth is at 1%. As shown in Fig. 2.5, the growth rate in carbon productivity needs to rise up to the orbit area.

We have just reviewed changing growth rates in labor productivity and carbon productivity, together with changing modes of economic growth and institutions. Organized by periods, they can be presented as Table 2.1. Apparently, the economy has functioned under mechanisms specific to each period. In the nineteenth century, the economy grew with expanding labor and environment consumption under institutions based on free competition. In the first half of the twentieth century, the economy stagnated with this mechanism malfunctioning. In the period of the postwar era to around 1970, the economy grew by improving labor productivity under the institutions of welfare states, while expanding consumption of the environment. This mechanism stopped functioning around 1970. Since then, alternative modes of growth have been sought. We also note that environmental productivity saw some improvements in the beginning of this period under state policies.

Table 2.1 Properties of economic growth by period

	Nineteenth century	First half of twentieth century	Postwar to around 1970	Around 1970 to today	Future (into 2050)
Economic growth	Mid	Low	High	Mid	?
Labor productivity growth	Low	Low	High	Mid	?
Carbon productivity growth	Low	Mid	Low	Mid	Very high (needed)
Mechanism of growth	Subsuming labor and environment		Improving labor productivity; subsuming environment		Improving productivity of both labor and environment?
Character of institutional coordination	Free competition		Welfare states	States' regulations in 1970s	Global competition?

When we look into the future, by adding its column to the table, we must put "very high" in the line of carbon-productivity growth, as explained above (see Fig. 2.5). Then, seeing the other lines, we have to face questions. Can the economy continue to grow? Is it compatible with high growth in carbon productivity, which combination we have never seen before? What kind of mechanism enables such growth? What kind of institutions can support it when global competition is prevailing?

This book seeks answers to these questions. To do this, we need to analyze the historically changing structure of economy and the environment in more detail, by delving into mechanisms of economic growth and institutional coordination. Let us proceed with this analysis by taking up Japanese history as an example. The fact that growth rates in carbon productivity underwent the largest change in Japan from 1950–1973 to 1973–1998 (see Fig. 2.5) indicates that Japan will provide the best example in analyzing the change at that time.

Theoretical frameworks that enable such an analysis are also required. In order to analyze historical changes with a focus on institutions, we consider a framework based on evolutionary and institutional economics. Thus, we conduct a theoretical study of a framework in Part II and then an empirical study of Japanese history in Part III. On these bases, in conclusion, we will explore future visions by coming back to the questions raised above.

Before closing this chapter, we will review the theoretical characteristics of our approach in Sect. 2.2, below.

2.2 Approaching the Study from an Evolutionary and Institutional Economics

2.2.1 Focus and Approach of the Analysis

This book approaches the issue of the relationship between economy and the environment, based on evolutionary and institutional economic theories. The intention is to understand the economy and the environment, not as one being superior to the other, but as interacting and coevolving things. For this reason, we use theories that underscore historical evolution and coordination by institutions, rather than presupposing an optimal equilibrium reached by an automatic adjustment mechanism of the market.

The various economic theories have their strong and weak points, and approaches should be chosen according to the nature of the issue and the purpose of the analysis. Looking at the issue of the economy and the environment, five widely recognized points can be raised: (a) the relationship between the economy and the environment has been evolving over a long period of time; (b) measures against environmental problems are determined largely by institutions; (c) environmental problems are essentially a manifestation of supply constraints from nature; (d) environmental measures may generate demand; and (e) environmental issues are linked to the industrial structure. Since it is not easy to reflect on all of these aspects at one time, pragmatic approaches need to choose which to focus on.

On the issue of the economic impacts of environmental measures, simulations using CGE (Computable General Equilibrium) and other models based on neoclassical theory have been attracting the attention of policy discussions. This approach provides detailed data that show how supply constraints affect the economy. On the other hand, the gap between demand and supply is assumed away, and the interaction between economy and institutions is not well explained.

In today's real world, the scientifically required level of environmental measures has not been introduced because of domestic and international political conditions, while policy ideas such as Green Growth or the Green New Deal have been attracting attention. In these circumstances, the aspects of institutions and demand are gaining more importance. Moreover, in the face of a historical crisis where the sustainability of the modern industrial civilization is at stake, one of the most important tasks is to understand the long-term evolution.

In order to approach the issue of economy and the environment while paying attention to these aspects of "long-term evolution," "institutions," and "demand," we will carry out the analysis based on evolutionary and institutional economic theories, in particular, *régulation* theory and post-Keynesian theory (inter alia, the Kaleckian model). Both of these theories place an importance on the role of institutional coordination in the functioning of the economy, and on the role of both demand and productivity in economic growth. Moreover, *régulation* theory provides a framework for analyzing the historical transformation of growth and institutions, using the concepts of mode of *régulation*, accumulation regime, and its crisis. The Kaleckian model has the strength of analyzing the relationship between costs and demand, as shown in the concept of "paradox of costs" by Rowthorn (1982). It also identifies different types of growth regimes, such as stagnationism and exhilarationism, which is beneficial in analyzing long-term structural changes. *Régulation* theory and the Kaleckian model are compatible: the Kaleckian model has been used in analyses related to *régulation* theory (e.g., Bowls and Boyer 1990).[3]

This book submits a framework to analyze the institutional coordination of economy and the environment using *régulation* theory as a basis, and suggests a model to better understand its impact on growth regimes by incorporating environmental costs into a typical Kaleckian model. This book also explores the possibility of future positive development of economy and the environment by referring to concepts from the wider arena of evolutionary economics. In order to build these elaborations as a consistent framework on a sound basis, we start by presenting a

[3]For example, Boyer (1986) mentioned that "regulation theory aims to give a renewed macroeconomic foundations that are more Kaleckian then Keynesian" and that it "shares three major ideas with the post-Keynesians."

concept of the socioeconomic system with environmental elements, by referring back to Polanyi and the surplus approach.

The theoretical framework presented here can be understood as an ecologically oriented integration of *régulation* and post-Keynesian theories, built on the basis of Polanyi's insight. This is also an effort to bridge the gap between environmental economics and evolutionary and institutional economics, aiming to make a contribution toward a possible "evolutionary environmental economics" or "ecological evolutionary economics."

2.2.2 Preceding Studies

At this juncture, let me touch upon where this study is located among preceding studies, in three areas: *régulation* theory, post-Keynesian theory, and environmental economics. (Readers not interested in academic contexts can skip to Part II [Chap. 3]).

Among economists in the *régulation* school, although Lipietz (1995, 1999) provided valuable insights and perspectives on the environmental issue, it is recently that works aiming at more analytical approaches, incorporating environmental issues into the core of the theory, have emerged (Becker and Raza 1999; Rousseau and Zuindeau 2007; Zuindeau 2007). These have recommended proceeding with analyses on specific forms of the relationship between the economy and the environment.[4] Among them, Becker and Raza (1999) have suggested that the relationship between economy and the environment be considered as a sixth institutional form in the framework of theory.

As Zuindeau (2007) has suggested, historical and comparative analyses need to be accumulated in order to understand temporally and spatially different forms of the relationship between economy and the environment. In connection with this idea, Élle et al. (2012) provided a comparative analysis of the environmental policies of OECD countries. Moreover, the methodologies of these analyses, including those with quantitative data, remain to be further developed. The studies presented in this book aim to contribute to the literature by proposing an analytical methodology that includes key indices of environmental costs, as well as by providing a historical analysis of the Japanese experience.

In the post-Keynesian school, although the search for possible synergies with ecological economics started early on (Gowdy 1991), progress was limited for a long time.[5] Recently, works have emerged that advocate developing

[4]There are several terms used for the relationship between economy and the environment, including "social relation to the nature," "ecological régulation" (Becker and Raza 1999), and "economic relation to the environment" (Zuindeau 2007).

[5]Among the post-Keynesian school in its broad sense, the Sraffian tradition had some notable literatures on environmental problems (e.g., Shefold 1997; Hosoda 1996).

macroeconomic theory for ecological economics on the basis of post-Keynesian theories (Kronenberg 2010; Rezai et al. 2013), and theoretical studies in this direction have been rapidly increasing (e.g., Holt et al. 2010; Fontana and Sawyer 2016; Guarini and Porcile 2016; Cahen-Fourot and Lavoie 2016).

The studies in this book, starting from 2012 (Okuma 2012, 2015, 2016), should be located within this trend. Those studies mentioned above explore various approaches, including one that incorporates the environment as a supply constraint, and one that uses carbon intensity as a variable in its model. This book suggests one simple method of modeling, by incorporating environmental costs into a typical Kaleckian model and thus analyzing the impacts of environmental measures. This can be understood as an angle on the theory that pays particular attention to the demand-side effects of environmental measures.

Environmental economics, in the broad sense, has a tradition not only of studies based on theories that presuppose market equilibrium (some call this environmental economics, in the narrow sense), but also those paying attention to institutions and social relations. One may go back to Kapp's (1950) concept of the "social costs of private enterprises" to find one of the roots of this tradition. In Japan, which was faced with severe industrial pollution in the 1960s, environmental studies based on the political economy were actively conducted (e.g., Tsuru 1972; Miyamoto 1989). Since the 1970s, ecological economics has attracted considerable attention, originating from Georgescu-Roegen's (1971) insight into the importance of the second law of thermodynamics (entropy law) in economics and being open to a variety of methodologies (Røpke 2005), including those approaches that focus on institutions and social relations (e.g., Norgaard 1994; Söderbaum 2000).

This book shares with these studies a basic approach of analyzing economy and the environment with attention to institutions and social relations. Moreover, it is influenced by the idea of coevolution of economy and the environment, proposed by Norgaard (1994), and explored by many scholars (e.g., Gowdy 1994). The contribution of this book will lie in exploring a way of detailed analysis, including both institutional and quantitative analyses, by proposing a theoretical framework based on *régulation* theory and post-Keynesian theory.

2.3 Concluding Remarks

This chapter, as a prologue to this book, has shared the main issues, in terms of historical perspectives, and has reviewed the characteristics of our theoretical approach.

The economy has been growing exponentially since the emergence of capitalism, and environmental burdens have also been increasing in the same trend. Meanwhile, the structure of economic growth (i.e., the growth regime) and the institutions supporting it has been changing over time. There was a period when labor input quantitatively expanded under free competition-oriented institutions (i.e., the nineteenth century), followed later by a period when consumption of the environment expanded while labor productivity was improved under welfare-state institutions (i.e., the postwar era until around 1970). There was also a period when productivity in terms of the environment was improved to some extent, due to strengthened environmental institutions (i.e., the 1970s). And now, the economy is faced with the limits of the earth's ecosystem and the science shows the need to drastically reduce environmental burdens. In the light of history, how would that be realized? What kind of growth structure would be possible then? These are the questions that we will try to answer in this book.

We approach these questions by using evolutionary and institutional economic theories, in particular, *régulation* theory and post-Keynesian theory. These theories have advantages in analytical viewpoints of long-term evolution, institutions, and demand. We build, herein, a theoretical framework for the analysis, and, by using it, carry out a historical analysis. This can be understood as an effort to bridge the gap between environmental economics and evolutionary and institutional economics.

This brings us to the end of the prologue. From Chap. 3, we will go into the main issue: a theoretical and empirical analysis of the relationship of economy and the environment.

References

Becker J, Raza W (1999) Theory of régulation and political ecology: an inevitable separation? Ambient Soc 5:5–20

Borden TA, Marland G, Andres RJ (2016) Global, regional, and national fossil-fuel CO_2 emissions. Carbon dioxide Information Analysis Center, Oak Ridge National Laboratory, U.S. Department of Energy, Oak Ridge. doi 10.3334/CDIAC/00001_V2016

Bowls S, Boyer R (1990) Wage, aggregate demand, and employment in an open economy: an empirical investigation. In: Epstain GA, Gintis HM (eds) Macroeconomic policy after the conservative era. Cambridge University Press, Cambridge

Boyer R (1986) La Théorie de la Régulation: Une analyse critique. La Découverte, Paris. English edition: Boyer R (1990) The regulation school: a critical introduction (trans: Charney C). Columbia University Press, New York

Cahen-Fourot L, Lavoie M (2016) Ecological monetary economics: a post-Keynesian critique. Ecol Econ 126:163–168

Élle L, Zuindeau B, Bécue M, Camara M, Douai A, Meunié A (2012) Approche régulationiste de la diversité des dispositifs institutionnels environnmentaux des pays de l'OCDE. Revue de la Régulation 12. http://regulation.revues.org/9951. Accessed 10 Dec 2016

Fontana G, Sawyer M (2016) Towards post-Keynesian ecological macroeconomics. Ecol Econ 121:186–195

Georgescu-Roegen N (1971) The entropy law and the economic process. Harvard University Press, Cambridge, MA

Gowdy JM (1991) Bioeconomics and post Keynesian economics: a search for common ground. Ecol Econ 3:77–87

Gowdy JM (1994) Coevolutionary economics: the economy, society and the environment. Kluwer, Boston

Guarini G, Porcile G (2016) Sustainability in a post-Keynesian growth model for an open economy. Ecol Econ 126:14–22

Holt RPF, Pressman S, Spash CL (eds) (2010) Post-Keynesian and ecological economics. Edward Elgar, Northampton
Hosoda E (1996) An environmental restriction and income distribution in a capitalist economy. Metroeconomica 47(3):236–265
IPCC (2014) Climate change 2014: mitigation of climate change. Cambridge University Press, Cambridge
Kapp KW (1950) The social costs of private enterprise. Harvard University Press, Cambridge, MA
Kronenberg T (2010) Finding common ground between ecological economics and post-Keynesian economics. Ecol Econ 69:1488–1494
Lipietz A (1995) Ecologie politique régulationniste ou économie de l'environnement? In: Boyer R, Saillard Y (eds) Théorie de la Régulation: L'état des saviors. La Découverte, Paris, pp 350–356
Lipietz A (1999) Qu'est-ce que l'écologie politique?: La grande transformation du XXIe siècle. La Découverte, Paris
Maddison A (2001) The world economy: a millennial perspective. OECD, Paris
Maddison A (2003) The world economy: historical statistics. OECD, Paris
Maddison A (2008) Statistics on world population, GDP and per capita GDP, 1–2008 AD. http://www.ggdc.net/maddison/oriindex.htm. Accessed 18 Dec 2016
Miyamoto K (1989) Environmental economics (in Japanese). Iwanami-shoten, Tokyo
Norgaard RB (1994) Development betrayed: the end of progress and a coevolutionary revisioning of the future. Routledge, New York
Okuma K (2012) An analytical framework for the relationship between environmental measures and economic growth based on the régulation theory: key concepts and a simple model. Evolut Inst Econ Rev 9(1):141–168
Okuma K (2015) Is green growth possible? Institutional and evolutionary economic analysis on the economic growth and environmental policy (in Japanese). Fujiwara-shoten, Tokyo
Okuma K (2016) Long-term transformation of the economy–environment nexus in Japan: a historical analysis of environmental institutions and growth regimes based on the regulation theory. Evolut Inst Econ Rev 13:217–237
Rezai A, Taylor L, Mechler R (2013) Ecological macroeconomics: An application to climate change. Ecol Econ 85:69–76
Røpke I (2005) Trends in the development of ecological economics from the late 1980s to the early 2000s. Ecol Econ 55:262–290
Rousseau S, Zuindeau B (2007) Théorie de la régulation et développement durable. Revue de la Régulation 1. https://regulation.revues.org/1298. Accessed 25 Nov 2016
Rowthorn R (1982) Demand, real wages and economic growth. Sutudi Economici 18:3–53
Shefold B (1997) Normal prices, technical change and accumulation. St. Martin's Press, New York
Söderbaum P (2000) Ecological economics. Earthscan, London
Tsuru S (1972) Political economy of pollution (in Japanese). Iwanami-shoten, Tokyo
Zuindeau B (2007) Régulation school and environment: theoretical proposals and avenues of research. Ecol Econ 62:281–290

Part II
Theoretical Analysis

Chapter 3
Socioeconomic System as Reproductions of Economy, Humans, and the Environment

In Part II, we proceed with our theoretical analyses of the relationship between economy and the environment. This chapter builds a common basis for them. This book aims to understand the relationship between economy and the environment, not as one side rules the other, but as both sides interact with each other. In order to obtain a theoretical basis for this task, we understand the socioeconomic system as being composed of three reproductions—economy, human, and the natural environment—and we analyze their relationships. In addition, in order to enable quantitative analysis, we define environmental costs, including the costs of environmental measures, as indices that reflect the status of the relationship between the reproductions of economy and environment. Thus we obtain a basis for detailed analysis in Chap. 5.

3.1 The Triple Reproductions and Their Relationships

3.1.1 Concept of the Triple Reproductions

To obtain a sound basis for a consistent framework, let us clarify a basic conception of the socioeconomic system. We do this by starting from the idea of Karl Polanyi and by referring to the surplus approach, together with the viewpoints of ecological economics.

Polanyi (1957), in his masterwork "The Great Transformation," perceived the economy as a historically changing process under two powers: the penetration of the market economy and the countermovement to protect society. He saw the economic crisis in the 1920s as a manifestation of the instability inherent to the market mechanism and recognized the New Deal, planned economies and Fascism as the results of various institutions' quests to control this instability. *Régulation* theory recognizes the capitalist economy as being necessarily coordinated by

K. Okuma, *The Evolving Relationship between Economy and Environment*,
Evolutionary Economics and Social Complexity Science 8,
DOI 10.1007/978-981-10-4100-6_3

institutions, and as being temporally and spatially variable. It demonstrates that the postwar high growth was a function of institutional coordination centering on a wage-labor nexus. These two views are consistent: both are based on a recognition of the inherent instability of the capitalist economy, the necessity of institutional coordination to control it, and possible crisis and structural change (Boyer and Hollingsworth 1997; Yamada 2007). Thus, it is beneficial to refer back to Polanyi's inspirations and consider the application of *régulation* theory.

Polanyi (1957) saw the fundamental cause of this instability as lying in the "fictitious commodities" of labor, land, and money. He argued that they are not commodities in the original sense because—with labor being human, land being nature, and money being a token of purchasing power—none of these are produced by humans for sale. However, in order for a self-regulating market to function, they need to be dealt with as if they were commodities. Due to this contradiction, human and nature are destined to be destroyed, and the economy becomes unstable (Polanyi 1957). From the viewpoint of this book, it is highlighted that Polanyi pointed to "land" or, in other words, to the "natural environment," as one of the three fictitious commodities, and clearly pointed to environmental degradation as one of the problems caused by an excessive market.

These ideas of Polanyi, which explain the fundamental causes of environmental degradations and their countermeasures within a historical perspective, provide us with a robust basis to analyze the relationship of economy and the environment. On this basis, let us try to develop a framework for economic analysis by referring to the surplus approach together with ecological economics.

The surplus approach is a tradition of economics that analyzes economic circulation as a "reproduction," while paying attention to the distribution of the "surplus" beyond maintaining the reproduction. This approach originated with the classical economists, including Quesnay, Ricard, and Marx, and has been developed by Leontief, Sraffa, etc. Since "sustainability" is basically synonymous with "continuity of reproduction," it will be beneficial to go back to the concept of reproduction when discussing the issue of sustainability. This approach, focusing on the distribution between profits and wages rather than presupposing market equilibrium, involves viewpoints around institutional coordination. Thus, it provides a basis for linking Polanyi's insights to detailed analysis, including mathematical formalization and quantitative analysis.

The surplus approach understands that a certain quantity of products must be used for the reproduction of capital equipment as well as for the reproduction of labor, in order to maintain economic activities, and that "surplus" beyond this amount is distributed among profits and wages above the minimum level. This distribution is determined by society's institutions. Thus, the socioeconomic system is recognized as being composed of two systems—the reproduction system of economy and the reproduction system of labor—the relation of which is coordinated by institutions (e.g., see Bortis [1996] for an explanation on this approach). This recognition is presented as Fig. 3.1 (Uemura 2007).

At this juncture, let us look at ecological economics. This school has emerged since the 1970s, with a central focus on the issue of sustainability. One of the roots

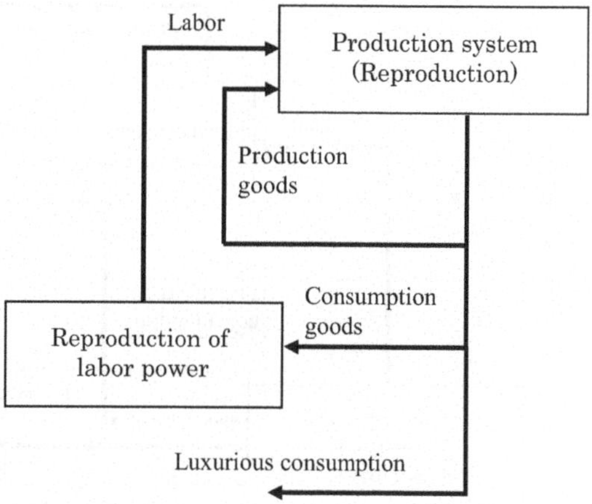

Fig. 3.1 Reproduction of socioeconomic system

of this school lies in the implications of the second law of thermodynamics (entropy law) to the economy, as suggested by Georgescu-Roegen (1971): the economy is not a circulate and timeless movement, but instead is an irreversible and evolutionary process that increases entropy. As such, it cannot be sustained without the input of low entropy, that is, natural resources and waste absorption services provided by the earth's ecosystem. On this basis, an emphasis on the embeddedness of the economy in nature was shared among the founders of this school of thought (Røpke 2005). Daly and Farley (2011) argue that the economy is a part of the finite ecosystem of the earth, although conventional economics sees nature as parts or sectors of the economy. This paradigm shift (a la Kuhn) or change in preanalytic vision (a la Schumpeter) is needed.[1]

These perspectives show that those economic theories that were developed without taking into account the essential role of the ecosystem need to be reconsidered, now that the scarcity of the earth's ecosystem has become evident. The ecosystem should be incorporated not as a series of mere categories of goods or services, but as a series of production factors of primary importance. In addition, these perspectives provide us with the viewpoint that natural resources and waste absorption services can be integrally analyzed as inputs of low entropy from the ecosystem.

By combining perceptions of the surplus approach and of ecological economics, as above, we obtain a recognition that both labor and the natural environment are reproduction systems distinct from the reproduction of the economy. Of these, labor has been the focus of economic theories so far, but the natural environment needs to be identified as an essential element within today's circumstances of growing ecological concerns. Based on this recognition, let us understand the socioeconomic

[1]This book, though placing importance on the view that the economy is a part of the earth's ecosystem (Daly and Farley 2011), also takes into account the huge influence of the economy in the real world. Thus, it sees economy and the environment as parallel systems.

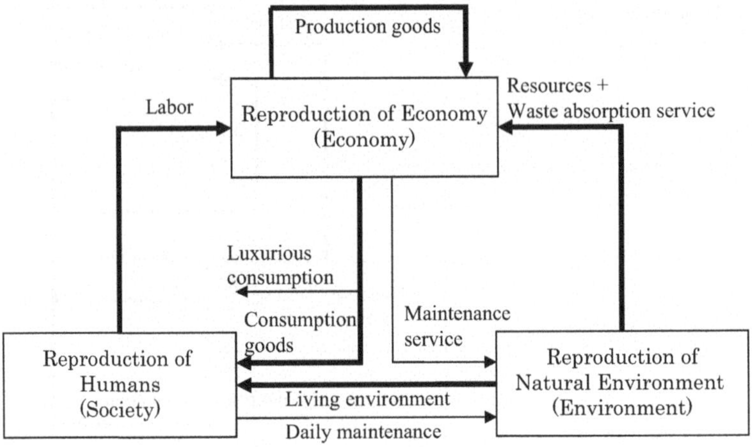

Fig. 3.2 Socioeconomic system as triple reproductions (Reproduced from Okuma 2012)

system as consisting of three subsystems: reproduction of the "economy" (within a narrow meaning), reproduction of "humans" (using a more general term for labor, in view of the balance of the three subsystems), and reproduction of the "natural environment." By extending Fig. 3.1, this recognition can be presented as Fig. 3.2.

The notion of a socioeconomic system consisting of three reproductions has been shown by Beaud (1997). He presented the concept of triple reproduction of the earth, humans, and capitalism as a way to understand the complex system of the world, and presented a historical vision stretching from the birth of human beings to an upcoming "great swing" *(le basculement)*. Being influenced by this school of thought, the book at hand aims to develop a concept of triple reproduction that can be used for analytical studies on the basis of economic theories.

3.1.2 Mechanisms and Relationships Among Reproductions

Let us analyze the mechanisms and basic relationships of these reproductions. The three reproductions of the socioeconomic system were, in the past, integrally functioning in close interrelation. Polanyi (1957) emphasized that the economy was originally embedded in society, but as the market economy prevailed, it gradually disembedded itself, began to function autonomously, and finally began to exercise ruling power over the society. We can understand that the reproduction of the economy, which was once embedded in the reproductions of humans and natural environment, has gradually been disembedding itself from them and functioning under its own mechanism.

Economy reproduction is a production system sustained by three categories of input: the production goods it produces, labor provided by human reproduction, and natural resources and waste absorption services provided by natural-environment reproduction. Products are distributed among profits, wages, and rents, which are appropriated for production goods, consumption goods, and the maintenance services of the natural environment.[2] We also call economy reproduction simply by the word "economy."

The natural environment is the reproduction system that is sustained by the productive capacity of nature itself, but that is partly supported by maintenance services from the economy and human society. Reproduction of the natural environment provides economy reproduction with natural resources and waste absorption services, and provides human reproduction with a living environment. We call these goods and services, provided by the reproduction of the natural environment, "environmental resources." When focusing on the function of providing these goods and services, the natural environment is often called "natural capital," as compared to manmade capital equipment. A part of the natural environment is owned under property rights and paid for with rents; a portion of these are in turn appropriated for maintenance services (e.g., fertilization and afforestation).[3] However, large parts of the natural environment are public goods and are not paid for with rents. When they are utilized beyond their reproductive capacity, they are degraded qualitatively and quantitatively. This degradation is often called the depreciation of natural capital, as compared to the depreciation of capital equipment (e.g., Daly and Farley 2011). The degradation of the natural environment, or depreciation of natural capital, causes environmental problems. We also call the reproduction of the natural environment simply "environment."

Human reproduction is sustained by the reproductive capacity of humans and society, together with the input of consumption goods and services from the production system and the earth's provision of the living environment (e.g., air and water). It provides the production system with labor and is paid for with wages, which are appropriated for consumption goods. We also call human reproduction simply "society," in contrast with economy and the environment.

The interaction of these three reproductions comprises the whole socioeconomic system. Relationships among these reproductions are not solely determined by the market, but rather coordinated by institutions.

---

[2]Investment in production goods is mainly covered by profits, purchase of consumption goods by wages, and purchase of maintenance services by rents, respectively. However, they do not completely correspond. For example, profits and rents are also used for luxury goods.

[3]We refer, by the term "rent," to the Ricardian rent, as well as various other forms of payment against the usage of the natural environment, including compensation for damages and newly introduced charge systems (e.g., tradable permits).

3.2 Economic Growth and Transformation of Reproductions

How can we understand economic growth when recognizing the socioeconomic system as above? Economic growth is no other than an expansion of the reproduction of economy. When production goods are input beyond the amount of depreciation, the stock of capital equipment increases and production capacity expands. Economic growth can be analyzed as this increase in capital stock, that is, capital accumulation.[4]

Now, the system of economy reproduction has a built-in mechanism to pursue growth. Under the market economy, products and production factors are exchanged as intermediated by money. Money functions not only as means of exchange but also as a means to store value, and thus becomes money capital. The inclination of this money capital to accumulate drives the reproduction of economy to expand. One may go back to Marx's (1867) formalization of M-C-M* for an explanation of this mechanism, though one can find its more direct expression in the recent phenomena of fluid speculative money, urging companies as well as states to grow.[5]

As can be seen in Fig. 3.2, economy reproduction will expand when inputs to it, that is, labor and environmental resources, increase. Since labor and environmental resources are not produced by the economy but by their own reproductions, the economy can increase their usage without increasing the provision of goods and services for their production. The economy, under the driving forces of growth and accumulation, tends to go in this direction.[6] When labor and environmental resources continue to be used in this manner, both human and nature reproductions are put under pressure. We can understand the interactions among the three reproductions as having an inherent tendency toward an expansion of the economy while society and the environment are degraded.

What will happen with the reproductions of humans and of the natural environment when economy reproduction continues to expand? As long as the scale of the reproductions of humans and the natural environment is large enough, compared to that of economy reproduction, the additional labor and environmental resources needed for the economy reproduction will be newly taken from them. More concretely, when a large population is sustained by the reproductive capacity of

---

[4]The approach of analyzing economic growth as capital accumulation dates back to classical scholars and was succeeded by the surplus approach, the post-Keynesian school, etc.

[5]Daly and Cobb (1994) also point to the nature of money as a root of the tendency to grow, stating that "money has a tendency to foster the exponential-growth culture... This happens for two reasons. First, by virtue of the fact that money can be created out of nothing and can grow forever, we tend to think that wealth... can also do these things. Second, with the historical shift from simple commodity production (C–M–C*) to capitalist circulation (M–C–M*) that money brought about, our attention turned to abstract exchange value, the accumulation of which appears to be unlimited...."

[6]Strictly speaking, when monetary circulation is taken into account, Say's law cannot be presupposed and demand for products may play an important role in accumulation. The model in Fig 3.2, being focused on the circulation of goods and services, does not deal with this mechanism, for the sake of simplicity. It will later be analyzed in Chaps. 5 and 6.

traditional communities, industries can employ additional labor forces. In terms of environmental resources, when economic activities are still small compared to the capacity of the regional or global ecosystem, they can exploit natural resources and emit wastes at will. This can be understood as an extensive expansion of economy reproduction by absorbing factors from other reproduction systems. In this case, the economy can obtain labor and environmental resources with fewer costs, without paying enough wages and rents to sustain the other reproduction systems.

When economic growth continues under the growth rate of positive value, the scale of economy reproduction grows exponentially. It expands extensively by subsuming more human reproduction and nature reproduction. On the other hand, the scale of nature reproduction has its limits determined by the earth. The scale of human reproduction, despite the intuition of Malthus, also has its limits, as can be seen in the history of developed countries. When economy reproduction expands beyond these limits, it becomes difficult to increase the input of labor and environmental resources. Thus, the structural change comes to be inevitable, from growth supported by increasing input to growth supported by improving productivity. In terms of labor, this is the "Lewisian Turning Point," that is, the phenomenon that economic growth that is supported by an unlimited supply of labor from outside a capitalist economy will reach its limit by using it up (Lewis 1954). For environmental resources, a similar structural change will also be inevitable.

Taking Japanese history, for example, the country's economic growth was supported by a supply of labor from agricultural areas until the Second World War. Yet it faced the Lewisian Turning Point in the 1960s, when the increase in the number of workers was curbed and wages started to rise. After that, growth came to be supported by improving productivity (Minami 1970). On the other hand, as Lewis (1954) mentioned, by resorting to immigration or capital exportation, an economy may be able to enjoy an unlimited supply of labor even after the turning point. In fact, one can see this phenomenon in the recent expanding frontiers into emerging economies and beyond.

Turning to environmental resources, there have been various types of exhaustion of natural resources at regional or national levels. The limits of waste absorption capacities have also emerged as industrial pollution problems. The former have been coped with mainly by importing resources from other regions. The latter have been managed by technical measures, such as the abatement of pollutants and waste treatment, though these have sometimes involved increases in energy consumption and thus CO_2 emissions, which may harm future generations. The limits of environmental resources have so far been dealt with via the spatial and temporal expansion of the acquisition of environmental resources, according to one interpretation. However, global environmental problems such as climate change have demonstrated that the consumption of environmental resources has already gone beyond the capacity of the earth's ecosystem as a whole. The economy can no longer rely on turning to other regions. Now that the extensive expansion of the use of environmental resources has reached its limit, structural change is inevitable. From growth relying on increasing quantity, the world must shift to that supported by rising productivity. We are, so to speak, facing a Lewisian Turning Point in terms of the environment.

In fact, the economy of humankind has not simply reached the limit. It has already gone beyond it. For example, according to the "Ecological Footprint," an indicator estimating the amount of land that is necessary to produce various kinds of resources, humankind's consumption already went beyond the earth's capacity in 1970s. This "Ecological overshoot" has been continuously increasing and reached 50% in 2008 (WWF 2012). Economy reproduction is consuming environmental resources beyond the reproductive capacity of nature reproduction; thus, the natural environment is being degraded and natural capital is being depreciated.

It is not possible for these reproductions to continue doing so forever. They must go through some forms of major change, sooner or later. Economy reproduction may be controlled to involve far smaller emissions and resource exploitations, or otherwise it will be forced to adapt to the degraded natural environment that involves harsh natural disaster. These changes, for economy reproduction, mean a reduced input of environmental resources and an increased leakage of maintenance services, which will affect accumulation and growth.

As explained above, the socioeconomic system, as triple reproductions, inherently has a contradictory mechanism in which economy reproduction tends to expand while degrading human and nature reproductions, though they are necessary for economy reproduction. This creates conflicts among the actors related to each reproduction, leading to the formulation of institutions to coordinate the interrelations among the three reproductions. The socioeconomic system evolves through this process.

In the relationship between economy and human reproduction, employment systems, such as lifetime employment with increasing wages and social security systems, were formulated. In the relationship between economy and nature reproduction, traditional rules of land management, regulations on pollutant emissions, and various rules on energy production/consumption and CO_2 reduction have been introduced and are currently developing.

Among these two areas, the former—institutional coordination between economy and human reproduction—is called the "wage-labor nexus" in *régulation* theory. This book focuses on the latter: institutional coordination between economy and the environment, or the "economy-environment nexus." In Chap. 5, we will discuss in detail the mechanism of institutional coordination within the economy-environment nexus.

3.3 Environmental Costs as Indices of the Economy-Environment Nexus

3.3.1 Costs of Environmental Measures

In analyzing the status of institutional coordination among the triple reproductions, it is beneficial to refer not only to qualitative information, but also to quantitative data. With regard to the wage-labor nexus, wage is a classic indicator. Turning to the economy-environment nexus, rent is the equivalent of wage. Moreover, the cost of environmental measures is a key indicator, as it represents the status of countermeasures taken under institutional coordination in monetary terms.

Since environmental costs, in particular the cost of environmental measures, tend to be scattered and merged into other costs in various sectors, it is important to clearly define and capture them. Let us do this by defining environmental measures in the framework of triple reproductions.

When the environment is degraded, the economy is forced, through institutional coordination, to produce goods and services that substitute for the environmental resources that were previously provided by the environment.[7] These include goods and services that substitute for natural resources (called "source function"), for waste absorption services (called "sink function"), and for both of these simultaneously. They also include goods and services that completely substitute environmental resources, and ones that can be used together with remaining environmental resources. For example, renewable energies, being produced by a combination of manmade equipment and the power of the nature, substitute both fossil fuels and CO_2 absorption services. Waste treatment services substitute a part of the absorption function that nature was providing. We call these environmental-resource-substituting goods and services (ESGSs).[8] Examples of ESGSs are shown in Table 3.1.

Although ESGSs are a kind of product of economic reproduction, they have a distinct character, in that they are produced with additional costs as substitutes for goods and services that were once freely or very cheaply available from the nature reproduction. In this sense, when analyzing the relationship between reproductions of economy and the natural environment, there is merit in treating them separately from other products (Fig. 3.3).

As described in Sect. 3.2, the economy, driven by capital accumulation, has a tendency to degrade the natural environment, leading to a need for ESGSs. Thus,

---

[7]There are different views on the substitutability of the natural environment, that is, ideas of "weak sustainability" and "strong sustainability." The former considers that natural capital can be substituted by manmade capital and sustainability is maintained if more manmade capital is accumulated than the natural capital is exhausted, while the latter sees no or little substitutability (e.g., Daly and Cobb 1994). This chapter proceeds with a presumption that there is a certain but limited level of substitutability.

[8]The concept of "environmental-resources-substituting goods and services (ESGS)" was initially presented by Okuma (2012). In the series of the System of Environmental-Economic Accounting (SEEA) that we will refer to in Chap. 4, SEEA 2003 used the concept of "environmental products," meaning a wide range of products including environmental protection activities, natural resource management and exploitation activities, environmentally beneficial activities, and minimization of natural hazards (United Nations et al. 2003). Recently, the SEEA Central Framework has introduced the concept of the "environmental goods and services sector (EGSS)," meaning sectors producing goods and services for purposes of environmental protection and resource management. The concept of the "environmental protection expenditure account (EPEA)" also continues to be used, focusing on the field of environmental protection in presenting a methodology to analyze expenditures (United Nations et al. 2014). The concept of ESGS, in this book, is close to EGSS in its scope. It differs, however, in that it uses a theoretical and simple definition of "goods and services that substitute environmental resources," and in that it enables a detailed analysis on expenditure-basis with referring to EPEA.

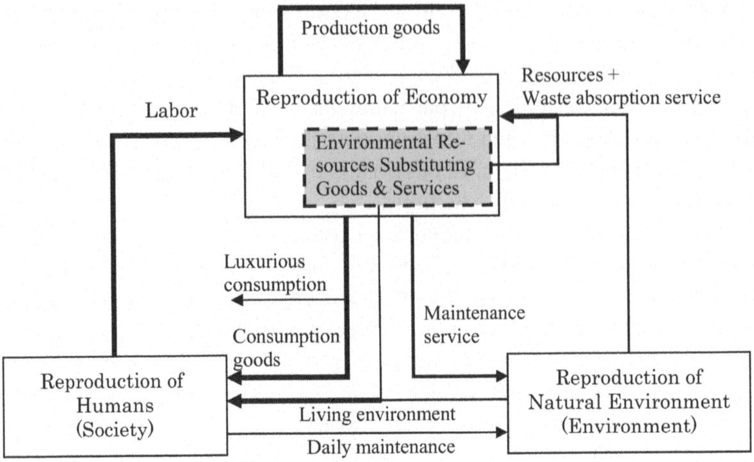

Fig. 3.3 Environmental measures as a substitute for environmental resources (Reproduced from Okuma 2012)

Table 3.1 Examples of environmental-resources-substituting goods and services (ESGSs) (Okuma 2012)

Source function (resources)	Additional input for exploitation of minerals due to their exhaustion Additional input for cultivation due to degraded fertility	Internal energy-saving service Renewable energy Resource recycling
Sink function (waste absorption)	Internal pollution control service Waste treatment service Adaptation to climate change	

we understand that the triple reproductions have a long-term tendency for structural change, involving a shrinking of the reproduction of the natural environment and an expanding consumption of ESGSs, although this tendency appears differently depending on the form taken by the economy-environment nexus.

Environmental resource substitutions are categorized into two types: those in economic reproduction and those in human reproduction. The former appear as intermediate consumption in the production processes. One typical example is the consumption of industrial waste management services. The input of facilities and labor for pollution abatement within companies can also be understood as the intermediate consumption of pollution abatement services by separating them from other inputs. The latter appear as final consumption by households. One typical example is the consumption of bottled water, made necessary by water pollution. Purchases of environmentally friendly goods such as eco-cars are also understood as substituting for pollution absorption services that nature had provided for free in the past.[9] We recognize activities of producing and consuming

[9] In this case, not the whole product but the additional cost is regarded as the ESGSs.

ESGSs as "environmental measures." Expenditures for ESGSs can be defined as costs of environmental measures.

3.3.2 Rents

The costs of environmental measures are closely related to rents. We have used the term *rent* in preceding sections without a clear definition. Now, let us clarify it. When one uses environmental resources that are covered by some kind of property rights, one must pay fees against their usage (e.g., land rents, payments for mining rights, payments for fishing rights, etc.). Moreover, when their usage degrades the natural environment and causes damages to someone, one may have to pay compensation against them (e.g., compensation for fishery damages, compensation for health hazards, etc.). These payments are made to those who have some sort of rights over the environmental resources and can be treated as rents in a wider sense.

Looking at the relationship between rents and the costs of environmental measures, when larger amounts of environmental resources are used, rents usually become higher—often through both larger rental fees and larger compensations—although they can be contained by environmental measures that substitute for environmental resources. Thus, rents and the costs of environmental measures are basically in a substitutive relationship with one another. On the other hand, they may overlap in some cases. For example, both (a) charges on wastewater that are paid to watershed management agencies and (b) payments to acquire emissions permits in tradable permits systems are fees for the usage of environmental resources as well as payments to bear the costs of environmental measures.

3.3.3 Latent Environmental Costs

So far, the costs of environmental measures and rents have been discussed. Another type of costs also requires attention when analyzing the relationship between economy and the environment. When the environmental resources in question are public goods, their usage does not involve rental fees or immediate compensations, though it may invoke some forms of social costs such as uncompensated health hazards or damages on future generations. We call such costs "latent environmental costs" in this book. They are latent because they are not paid by economy reproduction, though they do involve some form of costs borne by human reproduction. Environmental measures substituting the usage of environmental resources will contain an increase in latent environmental costs. Thus, the costs of environmental measures are in a substitutive relationship with latent environmental costs, as well as with rents.

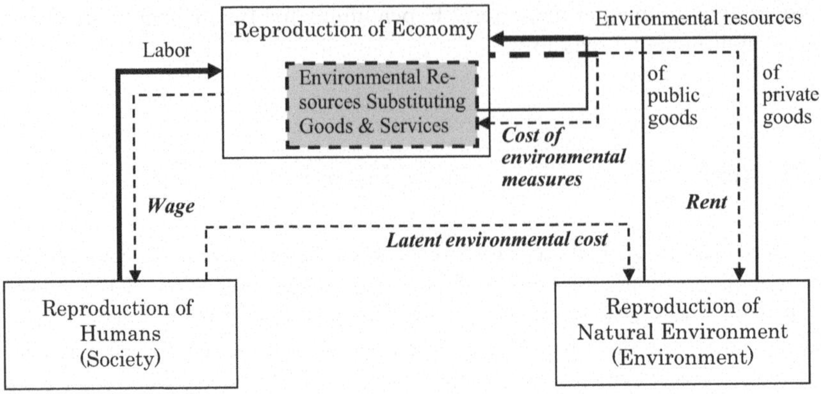

Fig. 3.4 Three types of environmental costs

We have discussed three types of environmental costs. In short, costs of environmental measures are payments for the consumption of ESGSs from the economy. Rents are payments for the consumption of environmental resources of private goods from the economy, and latent environmental costs are payments for the consumption of environmental resources of public goods that are not paid for by the economy but instead are borne by society. These relationships can be presented in the framework of triple reproductions, as in Fig. 3.4.[10]

There are three types of environmental costs: the cost of environmental measures, rent, and latent environmental costs all interact and change as the relationship between economy and the environment evolves. It is beneficial to trace and analyze them as key indices for analyzing the economy-environment nexus. The methodology of formalization to identify them within the macroeconomic circulation is discussed in Chap. 4.

3.4 Concluding Remarks

This chapter built a basic framework for the beginning of the theoretical analysis. We perceived the socioeconomic system as being comprised of interacting triple reproductions: reproduction of economy (economy in short), reproduction of humans (society), and reproduction of the natural environment (environment).

Economy reproduction has an inherent mechanism to grow by taking in larger quantities of factors of production from other reproductions, that is, labor and environmental resources. Such extensive growth must reach its limit someday.

[10]In this figure, the ESGSs used by human reproduction, as well as the costs accompanying them, are omitted for simplicity.

Just as we have experienced the Lewisian Turning Point in the labor aspect, some form of turning point is inevitable also in the aspect of the environment.

Relations among the three reproductions are coordinated by institutions and change over time. In tracing their status, quantitative indices are beneficial. As indices reflecting the status of the relationship between economy and the environment (economy-environment nexus), we focused on three types of environmental costs—the cost of environmental measures, rent, and latent environmental costs—and defined each.

These concepts work as a basis for the theoretical analysis of this book. In order to obtain a clearer understanding, as well as to enable quantitative analyses, we will mathematically formalize them in Chap. 4. We will also go on to discuss the dynamics of institutional coordination and the impacts on growth in Chap. 5 on the basis of the concepts in this chapter.

References

Beaud M (1997) Le Basculement du Monde: De la Terre, des hommes et du capitalism. La Découverte, Paris

Bortis H (1996) Notes on the surplus approach in political economy. In: Arestis P, Palma G, Sawyer M (eds) Capital controversy, post-Keynesian economics and the history of economic thought. Routledge, London, pp 11–23

Boyer R, Hollingsworth R (1997) From national embeddedness to spatial and institutional nestedness. In: Boyer R, Hollingsworth R (eds) Contemporary capitalism: the embeddedness of institutions. Cambridge University Press, Cambridge, pp 433–484

Daly H, Cobb JB (1994) For the common good; redirecting the economy toward community, the environment, and a sustainable future. Beacon Press, Boston

Daly H, Farley J (2011) Ecological economics: principles and applications. Island Press, Washington, DC

Georgescu-Roegen N (1971) The entropy law and the economic process. Harvard University Press, Cambridge, MA

Lewis WA (1954) Economic development with unlimited supplies of labour. Manchester Sch Econ Soc Stud 22: 139–191. Reprinted in Agarwala AN, Singh SP (eds) (1958) The economics of underdevelopment. Oxford University Press, London, pp 400–449

Marx K (1867) Das Kapital. Erster Band, Karl Max/ Friedrich Engels Werke, Band 23, Dietz Verlag

Minami R (1970) Turning point of Japanese economy (in Japanese). Soubunsha, Tokyo

Okuma K (2012) An analytical framework for the relationship between environmental measures and economic growth based on the régulation theory: key concepts and a simple model. Evolut Inst Econ Rev 9(1):141–168

Polanyi K (1957) Great transformation. Beacon Press, Boston

Røpke I (2005) Trends in the development of ecological economics from the late 1980s to the early 2000s. Ecol Econ 55:262–290

Uemura H (2007) Reproduction of socio-economic system and inequity in distribution (in Japanese). Polit Econ Q 43(4):5–15

United Nations, European Commission, IMF, OECD, World Bank (2003) Handbook of national accounting: integrated environmental and economic accounting 2003. http://unstats.un.org/unsd/envaccounting/pubs.asp. Accessed 25 Nov 2016

United Nations, European Union, FAO, IMF, OECD, World Bank (2014) System of environmental-economic accounting 2012: central framework. http://unstats.un.org/unsd/envaccounting/pubs.asp. Accessed 25 Nov 2016

WWF (2012) Living planet report 2012. WWF International, Gland

Yamada T (2007) Diversity in capitalist economy (in Japanese). Jpn J Comp Econ 44(1):15–28

Chapter 4
Formalizing Triple Reproductions and Environmental Costs

In this chapter, we formalize the concept of triple reproductions presented in Chap. 3 in order to obtain a clearer understanding. We also formalize the costs of environmental measures and incorporate them into the formula of triple reproductions. These formalizations will enable mathematical modeling (in Chap. 6), as well as quantitative analysis using indices (in Chap. 7).

4.1 Formalizing the Triple Reproductions as a Distribution Equation

As described in Chap. 3, we understand that the reproduction of economy is conducted via inputs of production goods, labor, and environmental resources, and that the products are distributed among profit, wage, and rent. By focusing on this production system, triple reproductions can be described as an equation of distribution with three dimensions (in gross terms), so that

$$pY = rpK + wL + \rho N \tag{4.1}$$

where Y is output, K is capital stock, L is labor input, N is consumption of environmental resources,[1] r is profit rate, w is money wage rate, ρ is money rent rate,[2] and p is price.

[1]This denotes the amount of the earth's source and sink functions consumed in the production process. Its measurement is an important subject of environmental studies, and some indicators have been proposed, such as the Ecological Footprint and the Material Flow Accounts, though accurate measurements are not possible yet.

[2]The rent rate is defined as total amount of rents divided by the total amount of consumption of environmental resources (N).

K. Okuma, *The Evolving Relationship between Economy and Environment*,
Evolutionary Economics and Social Complexity Science 8,
DOI 10.1007/978-981-10-4100-6_4

The surplus approach recognizes that the surplus, which is output minus its portion necessary for reproduction, is distributed among production factors through institutional intermediation. Subtracting from each term of Eq. 4.1 its portion necessary for reproduction (i.e., depreciation, in the case of capital equipment), normalizing by output, and assuming quantitative adjustment with variable capacity utilization, we modify it to

$$1 - d = r_n/uv + w_n/p\lambda + \rho_n/p\varepsilon \quad (4.2)$$

where d is the ratio of the portion of output necessary for the reproduction to total output (i.e., the ratio of depreciation, in a broad sense, to output); r_n, w_n, and ρ_n are profit rate, wage rate, and rent rate net from the portion necessary for reproduction of capital equipment, labor, and natural capital, respectively; $v = \bar{Y}/K$ is potential output–capital ratio (i.e., the ratio of output at full capacity utilization to capital); $u = Y/\bar{Y}$ is the rate of capacity utilization (defined as the ratio of output to potential output and $u \in (0, 1)$); λ is labor productivity; and $\varepsilon = Y/N$ is resource productivity.

This shows that surplus is distributed among net profit, net wage, and net rent. This can be illustrated as a distribution frontier plane in three-dimensional space (Fig. 4.1).[3] The economy exists in a particular place on the plane, which is largely determined by institutional coordination through conflicts over distributions.

Now, looking at the relationship between distribution and growth, we have the following equation (i.e., the Cambridge equation) under the classical assumption of saving only from profit.[4]

$$r_n = g_n/s_r \quad (4.3)$$

where g_n is net growth rate and s_r is propensity to save out of profit.

This relationship is proven to stand also when taking into consideration savings out of wages under a certain assumption (Pasinetti 1962). When taking into consideration savings out of rent, this relationship may become more complex, and has been a subject of theoretical studies (e.g., Baranzini and Scazzieri 1996). We develop a growth model in Chap. 6, assuming its application to resource-importing countries where rents go to payments for importation. Under such assumptions, Eq. 4.3 can still be regarded as effective.

When incorporating this relationship into Eq. 4.2 or Fig. 4.1, we see a trade-off relationship between growth rate and rent rate. However, if capacity utilization (u) or resource efficiency (ε) rise, the distribution frontier shifts outwards, releasing their trade-off.

---

[3]An expression of the economy in three-dimensional space with an environmental axis was previously shown by Hosoda (1994). He incorporated emission charge on waste (i.e., price of emission rights) to a growth model based on Sraffian tradition and described long-term equilibrium as a wage–profit–emission-charge surface in three-dimensional space.

[4]Under this assumption, the equation showing effective demand is $I = s_r\Pi$ where I is investment and Π is profit.By dividing both members by K, we obtain the Cambridge equation (Lavoie 2004).

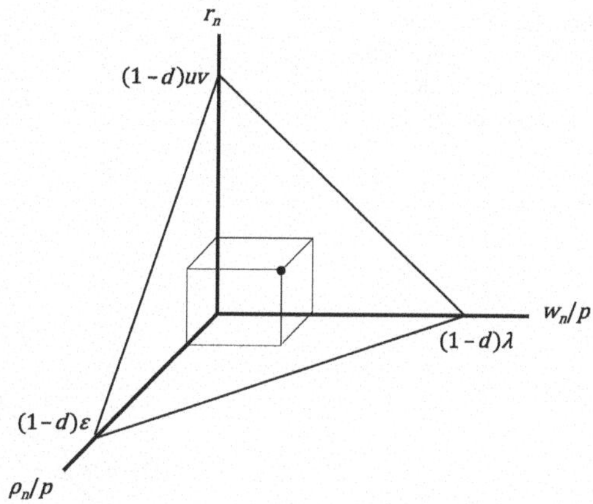

Fig. 4.1 Three-dimensional distribution model incorporating the environment

As explained in Chap. 3, a part of the natural environment of public goods is not paid for with rent, and its depreciation is not covered by it. If we incorporate this depreciation into Eq. 4.2, by subtracting it from net rent rate, we have

$$1 - d_g = r_n/uv + w_n/p\lambda + (\rho_n/p - d_e)/\varepsilon \tag{4.4}$$

where $d_g = d - d_e/\varepsilon$ is the ratio of genuine depreciation to output, and d_e is the depreciation of the natural capital of public goods per unit of consumption of environmental resources.

The natural capital of public goods, for example, forests with multifunctional roles and a stable climate, provides benefits to members of society, including future generations. If we assume that society as a whole has potential rights to it, then its depreciation ($-d_e$) can be regarded as a negative rent to society. Thus, the third term in the right side of Eq. 4.4 can be interpreted as rent to all rights-holders of the natural environment. These include not only people holding property rights on natural resources, but all of society as potential rights-holders on the natural capital of public goods.

When the natural capital of public goods is depreciated, environmental problems occur and some forms of social costs, such as health hazards on residents and the damages of disasters on future generations, will be generated. This depreciation of natural capital formally represents the latent environmental cost introduced in Sect. 3.3. This is a negative distribution to the society.

The genuine distribution frontier plane that incorporates this depreciation of natural capital shifts toward the origin, which is shown as the inner plane in Fig. 4.2. For example, if the apparent distribution in an economy is at A, but depreciation of natural capital d_e is generated, then the genuine distribution taking this into account should be located at B. This can be interpreted as a negative distribution to society in the form of latent environmental costs, enabling a larger distribution to profit and wage and thus a higher growth rate.

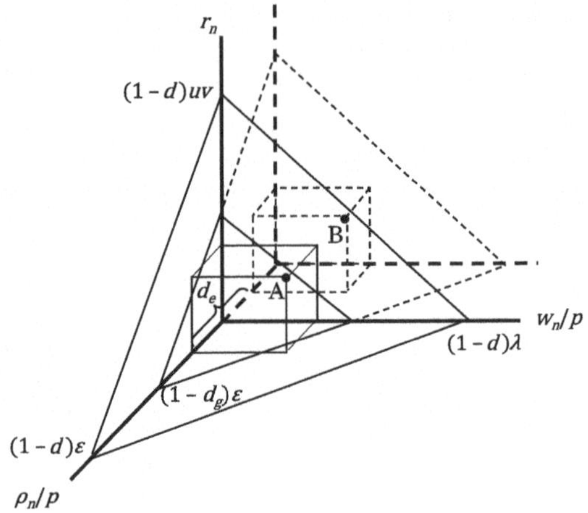

Fig. 4.2 Distribution model with depreciation of natural capital (Reproduced from Okuma 2012)

In this example, rent, including depreciation of natural capital, is negative and the economy is located in the area involving negative distributions to one of the production factors (presented by broken lines in Fig. 4.2). Negative distribution on a net basis represents the status where depreciation of production factors is not replenished, being unsustainable. Sooner or later, distribution has to change so that the depreciation is replenished, moving to the positive area on the plane (represented by solid lines in the figure).

Looking at the real world, as explained in Sect. 3.2, humankind's economic activities have already exceeded the reproductive capacity of the earth's ecosystem and are generating latent environmental costs to society. This cannot be continued forever. Sooner or later, rents in a wider sense have to arise in some form, such as compensation to victims or payments to recover the damaged environment.

In that case, surplus that could be distributed to profit and wage will be reduced as a direct effect. However, if capacity utilization or resource productivity rises, this may not occur. This relationship is analyzed in Chap. 6.

4.2 Formalizing the Cost of Environmental Measures

As discussed in Sect. 3.3, the cost of environmental measures is a key indicator in analyzing the economy-environment nexus. Since it is merged into other costs in various sectors, it is important that it be clearly defined.

Let us do this by referring to the System of Environmental-Economic Accounting (SEEA). SEEA is an accounting system developed by the United Nations Statistical Commission and other international organizations, on which three versions have been so far published: SEEA 1993, SEEA 2003 and the SEEA Central Framework (published in 2014). Methodologies for disaggregating environment-related activities and expenditures from the System of National Accounts (SNA) have been developed thorough SEEA 1993 and SEEA 2003, leading to the Environmental Protection Expenditure Accounts (EPEA). In addition, the former placed importance on the estimation of imputed environmental costs, while the latter focuses on hybrid accounts in physical and monetary terms, as well as on accounts for environmental assets. On these bases, with excluding accounting for degradation as well as examples and options, the SEEA Central Framework was compiled as the initial international environmental accounting standard (United Nations 1993; United Nations et al. 2003, 2014). In this section, we formalize the cost of environmental measures based on the methodology of EPEA, as adjusted to fit the purpose of our analysis. The methodology for estimating imputed costs will also be referred to in Chap. 7.

Environmental measures are implemented in various sectors, and their costs appear in the interrelations. We explore ways to grasp them in a simple form, in order to integrate them into the one-sector equation of distribution presented in Sect. 4.1 above. Focusing on activities that produce environmental-resources-substituting goods and services (ESGSs) (see Sect. 3.3), and referring to the idea of the supply and use table in SEEA (United Nations et al. 2003, 2014), we can describe economic interrelations using a two-sector I-O model consisting of the ESGS sector and the "production sector" that excludes it (Table 4.1).

In this model, the ESGS sector is defined as including activities that produce intermediate input into it, so that the box representing intermediate input from the production sector to the ESGS sector is empty.[5] The diagonal boxes are also empty, since each sector is conceived of as a consolidated process with a single product.[6] In order to analyze an open economy in a resource-importing country in Chap. 6, imports are divided into "rent equivalent" (the part of imports that corresponds to payments against the usage of environmental resources, most of which should be included in natural-resource imports) and "other imports," and are defined as an element of output together with the value addition.[7]

Intermediate input from the ESGS sector to the production sector (X_{ep}) is a variable that depends on institutional coordination within the economy-environment nexus.[8] An increase in X_{ep}, substituting input of environmental resources, reduces rent (ρN_d) or its equivalent in import (ρN_m), while it does not

[5]This definition is made by referring to the concept of vertical integration (Pasinetti 1973). However, investment is not transformed into annual intermediate input and is thus not vertically integrated in order to keep the model empirically traceable.

[6]Georgescu-Roegen (1971) suggested that, according to the analytical view of a process, each process of the I-O table should be associated with one product and diagonal boxes should be empty.

[7]The idea of a social accounting matrix (SAM) with import included in the output is shown in Taylor (2004).

[8]We note that this model assumes that capital and labor are not mutually substitutable and that environmental resources are substitutable by them. This is justified by our focus on the intentional substitution of environmental resources under institutional coordination.

Table 4.1 Environmental-resources-substituting goods and services (ESGSs) in I-O structure (Okuma 2012)

		Intermediate consumption			Final demand				
		Production sector	ESGS sector	Total	Consumption	Investment	Export	Total	Total
Intermediate inputs	Production sector	–	(Integrated)	–	pC_p	pI_p	pEX_p	pY	pY
	ESGS sector	p_eX_{ep}	–	p_eX_{ep}	$p_eC_e \approx 0$	$p_eI_e \approx 0$	$p_eEX_e \approx 0$	≈ 0	$p_eE \approx p_eX_{ep}$
	Total	p_eX_{ep}	–	p_eX_{ep}	$\approx pC_p$	$\approx pI_p$	$\approx pEX_p$	$\approx pY$	$pY + p_eE$
Imports	Rent equivalent	ρN_{mp}	ρN_{me}	ρN_m					
	Other imports	pM_p	pM_e	pM					
Values added	Wages	wL_p	wL_e	wL					
	Profits	rpK_p	rpK_e	rpK					
	Rents	ρN_{dp}	ρN_{de}	ρN_d					
Output (imports and values added)		$pY - p_eX_{ep}$	p_eE	$\approx pY$					
Total		pY	p_eE	$pY + p_eE$					

Note: Wage rate, profit rate, and rent rate are assumed to be uniform across sectors directly increase output (Y). Its value (p_eX_{ep}) can be regarded as the cost of environmental measures in the production system.

Here, the environmental-measure cost in the production system (p_eX_{ep}) includes costs for a company to procure environmental measures from other companies, as well as costs for environmental measures within a company as disaggregated from other activities.[9] In addition, in this simple model that abstracts from government sector, this cost can be regarded as including a considerable portion of government costs for environmental measures, since policies combining levies and subsidies on businesses (e.g., carbon tax and subsidies for energy saving, feed-in tariff systems for renewable energy, etc.) can be regarded as intermediate consumption of businesses relayed by the governments.

On the other hand, this model assumes away the costs of environmental measures in consumption (C_e), investment (I_e), and export (EX_e), for simplicity. This is based on the recognition that environmental-measure costs in consumption and export, being only additional values of so-called environmentally friendly products, have not shown such large increases as to change the aggregate quantity of consumption and export so far. This is also based on the classification in this model that large-scale investments, such as those for pollution abatement facilities, do not belong to investment in products of the ESGS sector but, instead, to investment by the ESGS sector in products of the production sector. However, in view of the increasing importance of countermeasures in the household sector as well as the possible development of policies involving governmental expenditures, further analysis of the costs in final demands is still to be pursued.

These assumptions make it possible to capture the costs of environmental measures consistently with economic theories, and to integrate them into a one-sector distribution equation. By dividing each factor of production into the portion used for production of ESGSs and that used for other production, under the assumption that profit rate, wage rate and rent rate are uniform across sectors, Eq. 4.1 (in gross terms) can be transformed into

$$pY = rpK_p + wL_p + \rho N_p + p_eE \tag{4.5}$$

with

$$p_eE = rpK_e + wL_e + \rho N_e \tag{4.6}$$

where E is consumption of ESGSs (corresponding to X_{ep}) and p_e is its price[10]; K_e, L_e, and N_e are the portions of factors used for production of ESGSs; K_p, L_p, and N_p

[9]SEEA emphasizes the importance of specifying and disaggregating ancillary activities within a company and presents methodologies for it (United Nations et al. 2003).

[10]Let us give brief consideration to the relative price of ESGSs and other products. If we assume production factors are utilized in the same proportion between these sectors (i.e., $K_p : L_p : N_p = K_e : L_e : N_e$), we have $p_e/p = Y/(Y+E)$. Here, in the current economy, $E \ll Y$. Therefore, we can understand that $p_e/p \approx 1$. With this understood, we proceed with the analysis using the one-sector model.

are the portions of factors used for other production (hereafter called "production capital," "production labor," and "production resources," respectively).

Normalizing by output, we transform Eq. 4.5 into

$$1 = r/uv_p + w/p\lambda_p + (\rho + \rho_e)/p\varepsilon_p \tag{4.7}$$

where $v_p = \bar{Y}/K_p$ is the ratio of potential output to production capital; $\lambda_p = Y/L_p$ is production-labor productivity; $\varepsilon_p = Y/N_p$ is production-resources productivity; and $\rho_e = p_e E/N_p$ is the cost of environmental measures per unit of consumption of production resources.

This formalizes the cost of environmental measures as an element of distribution. In this model, v_p and λ_p can be regarded as constant in relation to ρ_e, since an increase in E does not directly increase the output Y. Thus, an increase in ρ_e reduces r and/or w/p by raising the value of the third term. On the other hand, an increase in E, by substituting N_p, increases ε_p, which partly offsets these reductions. This relation can also be presented as the distribution frontier (Fig. 4.3). For example, when the economy is located in A, the addition of environmental measure costs (ρ_e/p) seems to move it to B. However, since resource efficiency rises from ε_{p1} to ε_{p2}, the distribution frontier shifts outward and the economy moves to C.

Moreover, the addition of environmental measure costs may increase demand and thus raise capacity utilization rate (u). In such a case, the distribution frontier shifts further outward and the economy may also move further.

These mechanisms will be analyzed in detail in Chap. 6.

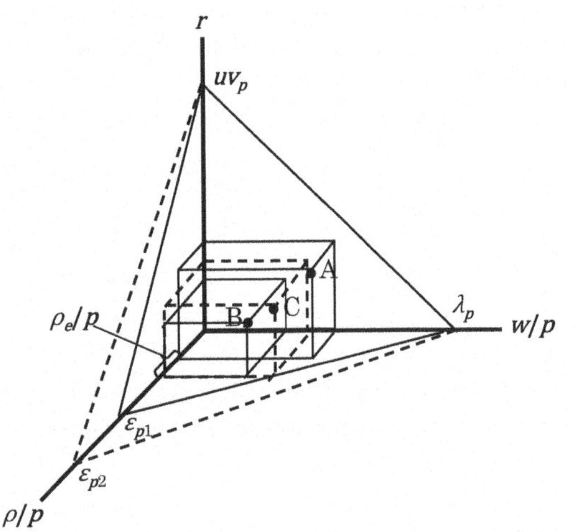

Fig. 4.3 Distribution model incorporating the cost of environmental measures

4.3 Concluding Remarks

This chapter has mathematically formalized the concepts shown in Chap. 3 in order to obtain a clearer understanding and to enable quantitative analyses based thereon. First, we presented the concept of triple reproductions as a three-dimensional equation of distribution among profit, wage, and rent. The natural capital of public goods is used without receiving rents and is depreciated. This depreciation can be regarded as a negative distribution to future generations, which corresponds to the latent environmental costs.

Second, we presented a methodology to identify and capture the costs of environmental measures in the context of economic transactions. Then, under some assumptions, we incorporated the cost of environmental measures into the three-dimensional equation of distribution as an element parallel to rent.

By locating environmental costs in the macro economy as above, it became possible to use them as quantitative indices with clear definitions, and to conduct analyses on economy and the environment by incorporating them into economic models.

Based on this chapter, we will conduct long-term estimations of environmental costs in Japan to trace the history of the economy-environment nexus (Chap. 7). We will also build a variant of the Kaleckian model, incorporating environmental costs to analyze the relationship between environmental measures and economic growth (Chap. 6).

References

Baranzini M, Scazzieri R (1996) Profit and rent in a model of capital accumulation and structural dynamics. In: Arestis P, Palma G, Sawyer M (eds) Capital controversy, post-Keynesian economics and the history of economic thought. Routlege, London, pp 121–132

Georgescu-Roegen N (1971) The entropy law and the economic process. Harvard University Press, Cambridge

Hosoda E (1994) Growth and distribution under an environmental restriction. Manch Sch Econ Soc Stud 62(1):60–80

Lavoie M (2004) L'économie postkeynésienne. La Découverte, Paris

Okuma K (2012) An analytical framework for the relationship between environmental measures and economic growth based on the régulation theory: key concepts and a simple model. EIER 9 (1):141–168

Pasinetti LL (1962) The rate of profit and income distribution in relation to the rate of economic growth. Rev Econ Stud 29:267–279

Pasinetti LL (1973) The notion of vertical integration in economic analysis. Metroeconomica 25:1–29

Taylor L (2004) Reconstructing macroeconomics. Harvard University Press, Cambridge

United Nations (1993) Integrated environmental and economic accounting: interim version. United Nations, New York

United Nations, European Commission, IMF, OECD, World Bank (2003) Handbook of national accounting: integrated environmental and economic accounting 2003. http://unstats.un.org/unsd/envaccounting/pubs.asp. Accessed 25 November 2016

United Nations, European Union, FAO, IMF, OECD, World Bank (2014) System of environmental-economic accounting 2012: central framework.. http://unstats.un.org/unsd/envaccounting/pubs.asp. Accessed 25 Nov 2016

Chapter 5
Institutional Coordination in the Economy-Environment Nexus and the Growth Regime

As discussed in Chap. 3, the socioeconomic system can be recognized as triple reproductions of economy, humans, and the natural environment that interact with one another, are coordinated by institutions, and evolve over time.

In order to understand the relationship between economy and the environment, it is necessary to analyze how institutional coordination between economy reproduction and nature reproduction works and how this coordination interacts with economic growth within the whole picture of the socioeconomic system. This chapter conceptually analyzes mechanisms of institutional coordination in the economy-environmental nexus and their impacts on the growth regime, using *régulation* theory as a basis.

5.1 Driving Forces of Institutional Coordination

5.1.1 Economy-Environment Nexus as the Sixth Institutional Form in Régulation *Theory*

To explore a theoretical framework for the analysis of institutional coordination in the economy-environment nexus, *régulation* theory provides us with a valuable basis. *Régulation* theory understands that the capitalist economy, although inherently involving a contradictory and instable nature, may continue to grow for a certain period of time as a result of institutional coordination. Under such stable growth, there must be a set of regularities that ensure a coherent progress of capital accumulation—referred to as an "accumulation regime" or a "growth regime"—and a set of rules of social relations that support this, called a "mode of *régulation*." Both of these can be diverse, depending on times and countries, and their temporally and spatially variable forms are analyzed in this approach (Boyer 1986; Yamada 1991).

K. Okuma, *The Evolving Relationship between Economy and Environment*,
Evolutionary Economics and Social Complexity Science 8,
DOI 10.1007/978-981-10-4100-6_5

The mode of *régulation* is made up of "institutional forms" in specific areas of institutional coordination, five of which are identified as: wage-labor nexus, monetary and financial regime, forms of competition, forms of the state, and position within the international regime. Among these five institutional forms, the first three are basic ones, while the latter two relate to the space in which they function (ibid.; Boyer 2000).

Specifying the three basic forms, in light of the triple reproductions in Chap. 3, we can understand that the wage-labor nexus corresponds to coordination between the human and economy reproductions, while the monetary and financial regime and forms of competition do to coordination within the economy reproduction. Here, in view of the essential role of reproduction of the natural environment and the current situation wherein its scarcity has become evident, the relationship between nature reproduction and economy reproduction should also be recognized as an important area of institutional coordination. Thus, we consider it rational to recognize the institutional coordination of the relationship between the nature and economy reproductions, that is, the economy-environment nexus, as the sixth institutional form.[1]

The economy-environment nexus is defined as the forms of utilization of the natural environment within socioeconomic systems, which are temporally and spatially variable depending on production technologies as well as on socially formulated institutions. The economy-environment nexus, interacting with other institutional forms, constitutes one element of the mode of *régulation*, and possibly affects the growth regime. Let us analyze the economy-environment nexus as one of the institutional forms, using the concepts of *régulation* theory.

5.1.2 Feedback Loop as a Driver of Institutional Coordination

In order to analyze institutional coordination in the economy-environment nexus, it is essential to clarify the mechanisms as to how it is formulated, by whom it is led, and by what it is driven. In so doing, it is beneficial to refer to the mechanisms in the wage-labor nexus, because the coordination of the reproductions of economy and the environment is, to some extent, parallel to the coordination of the reproductions of economy and humans.

As explained in Chap. 3, reproduction of economy, based on the market and capital, has a tendency to utilize a larger quantity of labor with a smaller quantity of wages, and a larger quantity of environmental resources with a smaller quantity of rents, in order to realize larger profits and accumulation. When they are overused beyond their reproductive capacity, the reproductions of humans and the environment are degraded.

[1]Becker and Raza (1999) and other researchers have previously suggested recognizing the relationship between economy and the environment as the sixth institutional form.

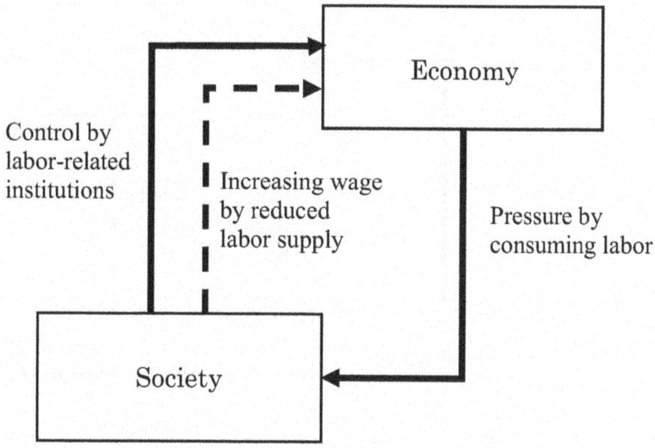

Fig. 5.1 Feedback related to labor

Then, in the wage-labor nexus (i.e., the relationship between the economy and human reproductions), reduced labor supply may lead to rising wage rates through market mechanisms. Moreover, workers begin labor movements to protect themselves and social institutions, including labor-management agreements and legal standards, are formulated. *Régulation* theory emphasizes that institutions are formulated as compromises through social conflicts.

On the basis of the composition of reproductions presented in Chap. 3, and by referring to the concept of feedback loops in general systems theory, these mechanisms can be described as in Fig. 5.1. Here we use the terms *Economy* and *Society* for simplicity, as well as to show our focus on pressure and feedback (instead of on the flow of goods and services).

In the economy-environment nexus, a degraded natural environment gives feedback to the economy similarly via two mechanisms, but through different routes. First, in the case of the natural environment of private goods, its degradation leads to a reduced supply of environmental resources or to increasing costs for its maintenance, and thus leads to rising rent rates through market mechanisms.

Second, in the case of the natural environment of public goods, its degradation leads to a reduced supply of environmental resources available to society, that is, a degraded living environment. This can be regarded as an incurred latent environmental cost, as explained in Chap. 3. Though their impacts are often suppressed for a while, when severe damages become evident, victims and their supporters in society claim countermeasures from those causing the degradation. This provokes social conflicts and leads to the formulation of environmental institutions. Thus, the mechanism of institutional coordination between economy and the environment works through society. Since the larger part of the environment is public goods, and since the first mechanism through the market seldom functions, the second mechanism—through institutions—plays a more important role.

On the basis of the concept of triple reproductions and referring to the concept of feedback, these two mechanisms can be presented as in Fig. 5.2. The economy and the environment, through these feedback loops, interact and change, and thus coevolve. Therefore, in order to understand the relationship between economy and the environment, it is important to analyze institutions while paying attention to interactions among economy, environment, and society.

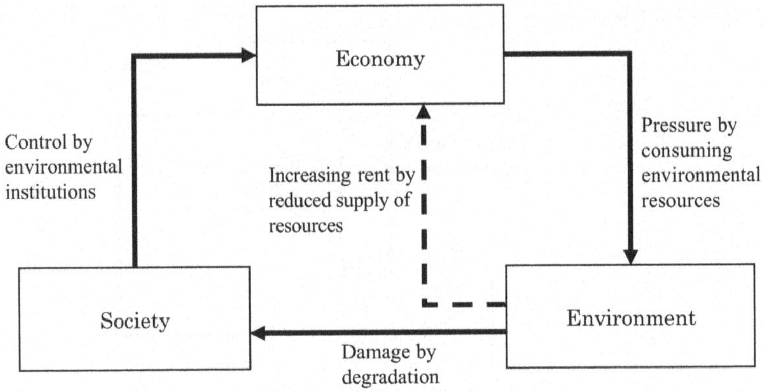

Fig. 5.2 Feedback related to the environment

5.1.3 *Mechanisms of Formulation of Institutions: Actors and Places*

As described above, feedback from the environment through society to the economy is the driving force for the formation of institutions in the economy-environment nexus. How, then, does this feedback mechanism work? Let us look into the details of this mechanism by focusing on actors and places.

In the most typical cases of environmental problems, actors suffering from pollution (such as residents) demand that the actors causing it (such as businesses) take countermeasures. The latter are often unwilling to take immediate actions. Thus, conflict arises. Environmental measures generate their costs, which are typically borne by polluting industries, while reducing the latent environmental costs borne by the victims of pollution. Thus the conflict is, in a sense, one over the distribution of environmental costs among actors.

We can therefore understand institutions for environmental measures as compromises formulated through conflicts among actors. Such institutions take various forms, including legal systems, agreements, and shared norms.

Actors take action not only as individuals or as corporations, but also as groups of members with shared interests. For example, victims of pollution may establish their organizations not just at local but also at national levels. Businesses may exert pressure through their industry associations. In addition to the actors with direct interests in the issue, other players who support them may strengthen the function of these actors. For example, governmental organizations (e.g., ministries) or specific groups of politicians may take actions in favor of one group of actors.[2] Scientists,

[2]It should be noted that a government play two-layered roles. Looking at a government as a whole, it works as a mechanism to legally institutionalize compromises among actors. Looking at governmental organizations separately, they work as actors representing specific interests in cooperation with other actors.

while providing scientific knowledge, may also take action on specific positions. Mass media often has a great impact by disseminating specific viewpoints.

The structure of these actors varies according to the type of problems and the characteristics of societies. This variable structure of actors, in particular, strength of actors who claim environmental measures, has great impacts on the nature of environmental institutions.

The characteristics of a particular environmental institution can be understood in relation to the structure of actors. For example, with regard to local industrial pollution, people directly suffering from the pollution are the main actors calling for environmental measures, and this leads to the introduction of strict regulations against pollution. On the other hand, in global environmental problems whose damages are spatially and temporally spread out, the power of actors calling for environmental measures tends to be weak, leading to the delayed introduction of countermeasures, as well as to relatively lax measures that may be of a voluntary and flexible nature.

In problems like these, where the damages appear to be vague or remote, the awareness of people who imagine or foresee damages to others and wish to take action to reduce them may generate actors for environmental measures. For example, NGOs with large memberships have been emerging on the basis of the ecological consciousness of citizens. These have influenced national policies, particularly in European states, as well as international negotiations of environmental treaties.

Let us next consider the places where institutions are formed. Institutions are formulated and formalized in particular spaces within societal governance. The most important place is the state, as emphasized by *régulation* theory. However, environmental problems arise on various scales, from local to global. For local problems, not only states but also communities and local governments play important roles. For global environmental problems, the formulation of institutions requires coordination at the national as well as at the international levels, including international organizations and conventions.

5.1.4 Spatial and Temporal Gaps of Coordination

In this connection, it should be noted that the actors and places involved in the formulation of the institutions mentioned above have their own spatial and temporal scales.

For example, in the case of industrial pollution, factories run by external capital can cause local health damages, for which effective measures often require policy decisions at the state level. In the case of transboundary pollution such as acid deposition, economic activities in other countries cause damages, for which effective measures cannot be implemented by a state. Climate change brings damages not only to any region, irrelevant of borders, but also to future generations beyond

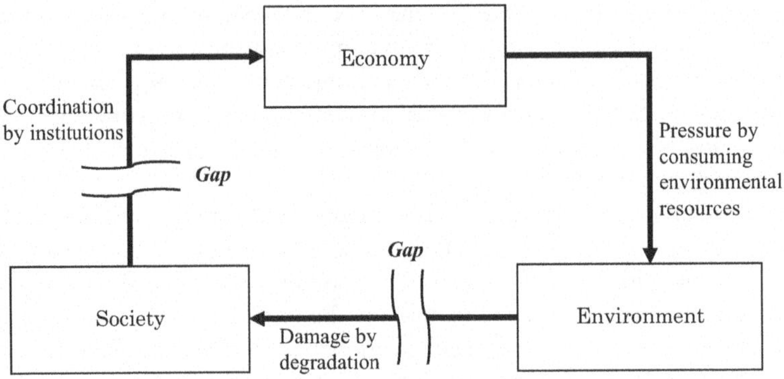

Fig. 5.3 Spatial and temporal gaps of coordination

the time horizon. We still, however, rely strongly on state-level measures due to the insufficiency of global institutions.

When there are such differences in the spatial or temporal scales of actors and places, coordination between them does not proceed well. This leads to delays in effecting countermeasures and aggravation of the damages.[3] We can understand this mechanism within the structure of the feedback loops explained above: that is, due to spatial and temporal gaps in scales of economy, environment, and society, feedback loops from environment to economy are not linked smoothly (Fig. 5.3). In this book, we call this phenomenon the "spatial and temporal gap of coordination."

When there are such gaps of coordination, a political process to fill the gaps is required before institutions are formulated. For example, in the case of local industrial pollution in Japan, the interests of local residents suffering from the pollution were initially almost neglected. Yet, after receiving support from the mass media and winning lawsuits, these interests finally came to be reflected in state policies. Various mechanisms of democracy played important roles in achieving this shift.

In the case of global environmental problems, scientists and environmental NGOs have called for countermeasures. Through international negotiations, treaties and conventions have been concluded on many issues, such as on the protection of the ozone layer. These are the fruits of human cognition to foresee future damages, as well as of the efforts of global governance.

Having said that, in view of the severity of the problems, the current development of institutions to address them is far from satisfactory. In the field of climate change, negotiations on the post-Kyoto framework stagnated, being stranded at COP15 in Copenhagen. The efforts were continued and finally an agreement was reached at COP21 in Paris. This constitutes very important progress, though it is not

[3]A similar idea has previously been established in environmental sociology. Funabashi (1998) pointed out that gaps between the "benefit zone" and the "victimized zone" worsen environmental problems.

a strict regime with legally binding obligation of emission reductions. In the field of biodiversity, though there is an international convention, effective frameworks have not yet been formulated to curb the decrease in the diversity of species.

Under these gaps in coordination, how can effective institutions be formulated? This is the question we now face.

5.2 Crisis and Institutional Change

5.2.1 Environmental Problems as a Structural Crisis

Next, let us consider the process of institutional change. We do this by referring to the concept of crisis in régulation theory.

Institutional forms in several areas constitute the mode of *régulation* of the socioeconomic system. When a mode of *règulation* works well to enhance an growth regime, stable economic growth is realized. When it stops working well, a crisis occurs. There are various levels of crises. A circulative crisis is a temporary phenomenon, but a structural crisis, in which the growth regime stops functioning, can put the institutional forms and the mode of *régulation* up for reconsideration (Boyer 1986).

A crisis may be caused by external shocks, although one caused by internal mechanisms has more serious consequences. When a mode of *règulation* continues functioning well, its coordination potential may be exhausted as a result of its very success, causing a structural crisis. This is the endogenous mechanism that leads from economic growth to crisis.[4] For example, the growth regime of Fordism, in the postwar golden era, reached the point of crisis by using up its potential for productivity improvement, putting up the compromise in the wage-labor nexus for reconsideration (ibid.).

When focusing on the economy-environment nexus, the above-mentioned growth regime of Fordism can be regarded as having an endogenous mechanism leading to crisis in its environmental aspects. Namely, the essence of this growth regime lies in rising productivity gained through mass production, involving the mass consumption of environmental resources. Sooner or later, this leads to increases in rent and other environmental costs. This mechanism also became evident in the form of the serious pollution and oil crises of the late 1960s and early 70s, which were calmed down by institutional coordination of pollution abatement and energy saving. However, this endogenous mechanism leading to environmental crisis has been continuing. Today, it has become evident once again as a crisis of a more structural nature, taking the form of the limits of the earth's ecosystem. This crisis has so far been emerging only gradually, but it will most

[4]The endogenous transformation of institutional forms through this type of mechanism is also called "endometabolism" (Boyer 2004, 2005).

probably be exacerbated in the future in various forms, such as irreversible changes to the environment (e.g., the unpredictable acceleration of climate change); concentrated severe damages on particular groups of people (e.g., vulnerable regions, future generations); and a world destabilized by environmental refugees. We are facing the chronic development of a major structural crisis.

Under this structural crisis, institutions within the economy-environment nexus, as well as the whole mode of *régulation,* cannot help but go through major changes. When thinking about the future of economy and the environment, a recognition of this structural crisis and the inevitable changes it will induce should have important implications.

5.2.2 *Coevolving Process of Institutional Change*

In such a crisis, how do institutional forms and modes of *régulation* change? A structural crisis provokes renewed conflicts among actors and, through political coordination, institutions are formulated and changed in the search for a mode of *ré gulation* that enables another growth regime. In this process, there is no ex ante guarantee that an institutional form in one area will be consistent with one in another area, nor that it will be compatible with a new growth regime. Instead, institutional forms are ex-post adjusted to each other and to the accumulation regime, which is a coevolution of institutions and the economy (Boyer 2004, 2005).

Thus, institutions formulated in each area are stable if compatible with the mode of *régulation* and the growth regime, but will otherwise be unstable under pressures to change. When new institutional coordination is explored in the economy-environment nexus, it is inevitably checked against compatibility with the growth regime. This recognition has implications when considering the feasibility of new institutions in the economy-environment nexus.

In addition, the above-mentioned understanding of institutional change leads to the notion that institutions and the economy are not built according to a certain plan, but rather are formulated through an ongoing process of exploration and experimentation. This is also an important viewpoint when considering future policies.

5.2.3 *Institutional Hierarchy and Institutional Complementarity*

Institutions change through interactions with other fields of institutional forms, as well as with the growth regime. This interaction can be analyzed in light of the concepts of "institutional hierarchy" and "institutional complementarity." Institutional hierarchy refers to a state where a particular institutional domain imposes its logic on the others, lending its style to a mode of *régulation*. Institutional complementarity refers to a state in which the viability of institutions in one domain is supported by those of others, constituting a resilient and effective architecture

(Amable 2003; Boyer 2004, 2005). The concept of institutional complementarity has been widely used in institutional economics since it was proposed by Aoki (1996). The *régulation* school has been emphasizing the concept of institutional hierarchy, under its attention to the dynamics of institutional change.

The transformation of an institutional form that is dominant in an institutional hierarchy urges other institutional forms to change. The hierarchy may be reversed in history. The logic of the institutional form that is then ranked higher will change other institutional forms (Boyer 2004, 2005).

For example, the wage-labor nexus was dominant in the postwar high-growth era, and its logic influenced other institutional forms. However, other institutional forms, that is, "position within the international regime" and "monetary and financial regime," took its place and became dominant in the 1990s. Since then, the globalization of the economy and the financialization of corporate governance have had great impact also on the wage-labor nexus (Boyer 2000).

When analyzing the formulation and change of institutions within the economy-environment nexus, it is beneficial to refer to the concepts of institutional complementarity and hierarchy. So far, the economy-environment nexus generally has been located at a lower level of the institutional hierarchy, and its particular forms may be understood from the viewpoint of its complementarity with other, higher-level institutional forms. For example, in the postwar high-growth era, the wage-labor nexus was characterized by higher wage levels in response to workers' demands, and the nature of nation states was described as "Keynesian welfare states" (Jessop 2002). Strict anti-pollution regulations, which were introduced by states in response to local residents' demands, can be seen as compatible with these institutional forms. On the other hand, in later years, an international regime centering on global competition became dominant in the institutional hierarchy, influencing other institutional forms. We see a general tendency toward voluntary and flexible nature of environmental institutions, which may be better understood within a viewpoint of complementarity with the competitive international regime.

On the other hand, if environmental constraints become severer and the above-mentioned structural crisis becomes more pressing, the economy-environment nexus may come to be ranked higher in the institutional hierarchy. It may then begin to influence other institutional forms, as well as the whole mode of *ré gulation*.

In addition, the recognition of complementarity between different domains of institutions leads to the notion that social problems in various areas are interlinked. Labor problems (such as increasing informal employment) and environmental problems (such as a lack of effective regulations) are both related to the competitive international regime, which is currently dominant in the institutional hierarchy and therefore imposes its logic on other institutions. Recently, the idea has emerged that social issues and environmental issues should be resolved in an integrated manner; this notion is supported by the recognition of institutional complementarity.

5.3 Interactions with the Growth Regime

As described in the preceding section, institutional coordination in the economy-environment nexus is formulated and changed through interactions with other institutional forms as well as with the growth regime. Interaction between the economy-environment nexus and the growth regime is of great importance when analyzing the relationship between economy and the environment. This section will closely analyze said interaction.

5.3.1 Growth Regime and the Economy-Environment Nexus

As the first step, let us review the basic structure of the growth regime (Fig. 5.4). The growth regime is analyzed in terms of production and productivity. Productivity rises not only through exogenous innovations, but also through endogenous mechanisms such as dynamic increasing returns on the scale of production, as well as technical progress induced by investment. This mechanism is represented, in the figure, as two arrows from the lower right ("Production") and center ("Investment") to the upper left ("productivity,") and is called the "productivity regime." Improved productivity increases surpluses, which are distributed between wage and profit under a certain institutional coordination, leading to increases in consumption and investment and, thus, demand. This is presented as arrows running from the upper left ("Productivity") through "Consumption" or "Investment" to the lower right ("Production,") and is called the "demand regime". Companies normally operate with some capacity of their facilities reserved (i.e., not at full capacity-utilization). In such a state of economy, production is determined by demand. Thus, improved

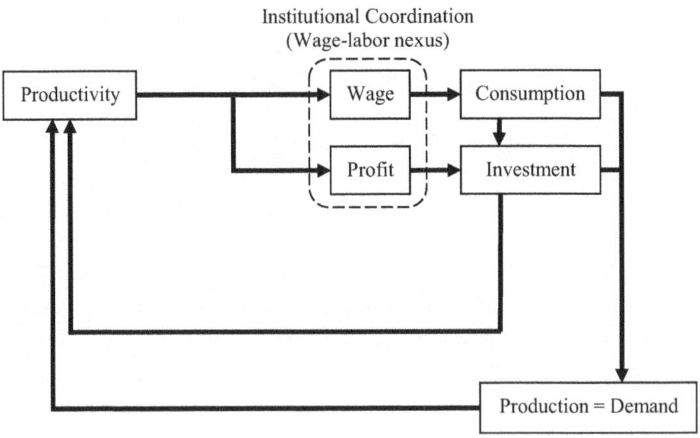

Fig. 5.4 Basic structure of the growth regime

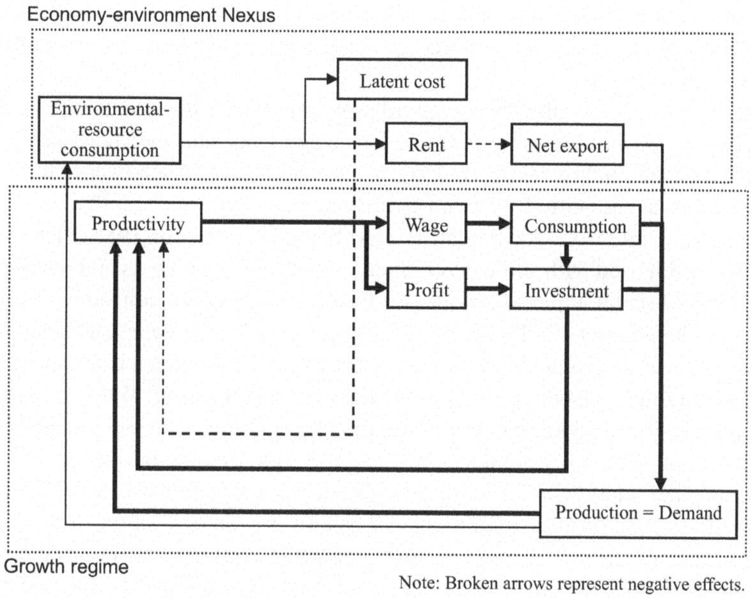

Fig. 5.5 Growth regime and economy-environment nexus

productivity increases demand and production through the demand regime, which in turn improves productivity through the productivity regime.

During the postwar era of high growth, these two effects worked in a cumulative causation, supported by institutional coordination centering on the wage-labor nexus, in what is generally called the Fordist regime of accumulation (Boyer 1986). It should be noted that there have been and can be other forms of growth mechanisms. For example, a growth regime driven by finance emerged in the United States in the 1990s (Boyer 2000).

The growth regime and the economy-environment nexus are interlinked through multiple routes. Let us analyze them by adding the economy-environment nexus to the basic structure of growth regime, paying attention to the environmental costs defined in Chap. 3 (Fig. 5.5). Here, it should be noted that this diagram of the growth regime is used as a basic frame upon which to identify the linkages, even though its mechanisms are currently not working effectively as in the Fordist era.

Production involves the consumption of environmental resources, generating rent (in the form of costs of natural resources), and latent environmental cost (in the form of environmental degradation imposing costs on society). They can be located in parallel with wage and profit as elements of distribution.

When production increases, the consumption of environmental resources also increases (as presented by the arrow from the lower right to the upper left, in Fig. 5.5). If it is within the reproductive capacity of the natural environment, then rent remains at a low level and the economy-environment nexus does not have visible impacts on the growth regime. Even when it goes beyond the ecological capacity, the same conditions can be maintained by generating latent environmental costs. Thus, production may continue growing with an expanding consumption of environmental resources.

Règulation theory calls the accumulation regime in the nineteenth century, characterized by an increasing input of low-wage labor and the successive establishment of heavy industries, "extensive accumulation." The late twentieth century regime that was supported by continuously rising labor productivity, in turn, is referred to as "intensive accumulation" (Aglietta 1976; Boyer 1986). These concepts have been used with some divergence, depending on contexts and researchers. When focused on the input of production factors, an accumulation supported by an increase in its amount can be regarded as "extensive," while one supported by an improvement in its productivity can be "intensive." This enables us to apply these concepts not only to labor but also to the environmental aspect. When the input of environmental resources expands without their rents rising, as mentioned above, the growth regime can be regarded as extensive in its environmental aspect.

On the other hand, when the consumption of environmental resources continues to expand, the long-term trend of rents will be upward due to resource depletion. An increase in rents, in the case of resource-importing countries, works as a leakage from the economy, which reduces net export and thus demand (presented as the broken arrow from "Rent" to "Net export" that connects with the arrow to "Demand" in the figure). In resource-producing countries, its effects depend on the properties of specific economies, such as the propensity to save from rents.

In addition, when the natural environment continues to be degraded, it will end up causing damages not only on residents' health but also on production activities, for it is the basis of both. For example, recent severe pollution in China is said to have affected agriculture by degrading the soil and water, and to have even impacted the manufacturing and service industries by damaging workers' health. Moreover, when climate change intensifies natural disasters, greater expenses and labor forces must be spared for disaster management and recovery, which in turn reduces productivity of the economy as a whole. This can be recognized as causation: the latent environmental cost (i.e. depletion of the natural capital) affects labor productivity (presented as the broken arrow from "Latent environmental cost" to "Productivity").

These two effects mean that a growth regime supported by continuously expanding resource consumption, such as Fordism, has inner dynamics that can undermine its own basis and lead to a crisis of the regime.

Looking at the current state of the world, the scale of humankind's economic activities is said to have gone beyond the limits of the earth's ecosystem (see Sect. 3.2), implying that a rise in rents or a decline in productivity, as explained above, will occur sooner or later. This can be regarded as a delayed emergence of an endogenous crisis of the growth regime that has an extensive nature in environmental aspect.

5.3.2 *Multiple Effects of Environmental Measures on the Growth Regime*

As discussed in Sect. 5.1, when the consumption of environmental resources continues to expand, both rents and latent environmental costs increase. In response, environmental measures are strengthened and the costs of environmental measures increase. This is an institutional coordination among rent, latent environmental cost, and the cost of environmental measures, represented in Fig. 5.6 as an upper frame. An increase in the cost of environmental measures impacts the growth regime through multiple routes, either via the demand regime or the productivity regime. Let us look at how these routes work for each regime.

5.3.2.1 Effects on the Demand Regime

The impacts on the demand regime are multifaceted. First, environmental measures improve resource productivity and thus reduce rents (presented as the route through

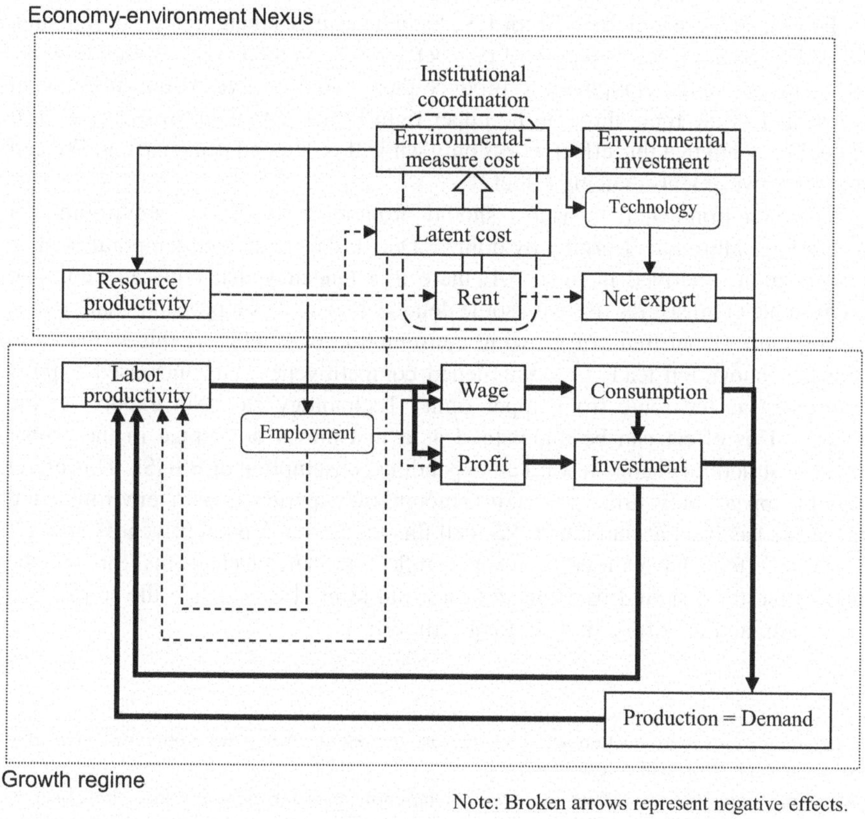

Fig. 5.6 Effects of environmental measures on the growth regime

the upper-left ["Resource productivity"] in Fig. 5.6). This leads to increased net exports through reduced resource importation, in the case of resource-importing countries. In this book, we will call this the "resource-saving effect."

Second, it has both positive and negative impacts on demand through a change in distribution. An increase in the cost of environmental measures involves larger labor inputs for the production of environmental-resources-substituting goods and services (ESGSs), while not directly increasing the total added value, in the case of environmental measures in the production activities.[5] This is reflected in the increased total wages and reduced profit, when assuming a constant real wage rate under quantitative adjustments (presented as the routes through "Employment" to "Wage" and "Profit" in the figure). Here, increased total wages lead to increased consumption, while reduced profit leads to reduced investment. This is a combined effect of cost on demand through distribution. We call this the "cost-demand effect."

Third, in the case of environmental measures in consumption activities, an increase in the production and consumption of ESGSs may increase the final demand and thus the output of the economy. However, this happens only when large-scale increases occur, in which the propensity to consume as a whole rises and the total amount of consumption increases (omitted in the figure).

Fourth, an increased demand for ESGSs induces investment in their production. Since ESGSs are a new category of products, growth in their consumption requires new sorts of capital equipment to produce them and thus gives rise to investment (presented as the route through the upper right ["Environmental investment"]). It should be noted that this effect works only while this demand is increasing. We call this the "investment-inducing effect."

Fifth, environmental measures should promote innovation in environmental technologies through "learning by doing." Due to the spatial and temporal gaps in coordination described in Sect. 5.1, there is a tendency that rents and costs of environmental measures rise with some delay, which makes it probable that there is a long-term global trend of growing consumption of ESGSs. If this is the case, induced innovation leads to strengthened competitiveness and increased exports (presented as the route from upper right "Technology" to "Net export" in the figure). This effect can be understood as a first-mover advantage in the global trend of structural change toward an expanding consumption of ESGSs. This effect should appear only after a certain amount of experience with environmental measures has been accumulated. We call this the "export competitiveness effect."

These effects have varied time scales reflecting their mechanisms. Simply, the first to the third should be understood as mid-term effects, while the fourth is a short-term and the fifth a mid- to long-term effect.[6]

[5]Countermeasures in production activities increase the intermediate consumption of ESGSs, but do not increase their final consumption.

[6]More precisely, the first effect involves a long-term character as well, since the effect of environmental measures to reduce resource consumption is reinforced by technological development and the accumulation of capital equipment.

5.3.2.2 Effects on the Productivity Regime

Impacts on the productivity regime are also two-sided. As a direct effect, environmental measures in the production system reduce labor productivity, since they require additional labor inputs to produce ESGSs for intermediate consumption (presented as the route from "Employment," in the middle, to the upper left "Labor productivity" in the figure). Businesses often oppose strengthening environmental measures, arguing that it will raise costs and affect the economy. Their arguments correspond to this effect of reducing productivity, together with the effect of reducing profit as a part of the cost-demand effect explained above.

On the other hand, when environmental measures enhance natural capital, it will contribute to higher labor productivity in the whole economy (presented as the route running from "Resource productivity" through "Latent environmental cost" to "Labor productivity," in the figure). For example, severe pollution may lower labor productivity, while environmental measures can alleviate it. Clean and fertile ecosystem preserved by environmental measures may contribute to productive agriculture, fisheries, and possibly tourism. Here it should be noted that the place where this effect appears may not be the same as where the environmental measures are taken, as explained in Sect. 5.1 regarding spatial and temporal gaps in coordination. In addition, since natural capital can hardly accumulate immediately, this effect should be considered as mid- to long-term one.

5.3.3 Analyzing the Synthetic Effect

The multiple effects described above work in synthesis and impact the growth regime either positively or negatively, depending on the state of the economy and the nature of environmental measures. Let us look at this synthetic effect.

5.3.3.1 Paradox of Costs for Environmental Measures

When focusing on the demand regime, there are many routes through which an increase in the cost of environmental measures leads to an increase in demand, as analyzed in Sect. 5.3.2. Since there are also some routes where it leads to a decrease in demand, we cannot derive a universal result; the synthetic effects may differ depending on conditions. However, it can safely be said that an increase in the cost of environmental measures will raise demand with high probability, when some conditions are met: that is, if this takes place in a resource-importing country where environmental measures can reduce importation; under economic conditions in which consumption is responsive to wage income and investment is more responsive to demand than to profit; and/or in an industrial country where innovation in environmental technologies may enhance export competitiveness.

Rowthorn (1982) theoretically demonstrated that higher wage rates may lead to higher profit and growth rates, calling this phenomenon "the paradox of costs." The cost-demand effect with positive impacts in the previous section corresponds to this paradox of costs. The cost of environmental measures, with the additional effects of resource-saving, investment-inducement and export competitiveness, as in the previous section, will increase demand in wider circumstances. We call this phenomenon "the paradox of costs for environmental measures."

This is a paradoxical effect in which environmental measures, though raising costs as a direct effect, also add to demand and enhance the growth of the whole economy. Recognition of this effect should have important policy implications, especially when proposed policies face concerns about the economic impact of their costs. The ideas of Green Growth have been drawing the interest of policy-makers since the global economic crisis. This concept of the paradox of costs for environmental measures theoretically explains the mechanism through which Green Growth can be realized.

How and when this mechanism works can be more clearly shown through mathematical models. We will analyze this mechanism in detail, using a variant of the Kaleckian model, in Chap. 6.

5.3.3.2 Long-Term Effects on the Productivity Regime

The growth regime is composed of the demand regime and the productivity regime. The demand regime alone, even if working effectively, will not be able to maintain stable growth in the long run, as stagnant productivity will depress the surplus that can be distributed and thus the whole demand. In addition, in the case of economies with decreasing populations, labor supply constraints may become a determining factor of the economy in the future.

The cost of environmental measures impacts the productivity regime either positively or negatively, as described in Sect. 5.3.2. Directly, it lowers labor productivity by requiring additional labor input to produce intermediate consumption goods. On the other hand, in the longer term, it may improve labor productivity by enhancing the natural capital. Moreover, when production increases through the paradox of costs in the demand regime, labor productivity rises through induced innovations and enlarged working opportunities, that is, dynamic increasing returns to scale. The combined effect of these positive and negative impacts depends on the state of the economy and the nature of the environmental measures, as well as on the future role of the natural capital in production.

In this context of considering supply constraints in the long run, we should recall that environmental resources are also an essential factor of production, based on the notion of triple reproductions, and thus they need to be taken into account together with labor and capital. Among these three factors of production, environmental resources have reached the ultimate limits of the earth's ecosystem in terms of quantity, while capital and even labor can still increase in the long run. Though the supply constraints of environmental resources have not yet become fully apparent, they will sooner or later severely affect the growth regime, whether through rising rents as resource costs or through the materialization of latent environmental costs (e.g., costs incurred due to natural disasters), unless resource productivity is drastically improved.

The economy may be constrained by any of these three factors of production, and the determining factor may change from one to another over time. This shift in the determining factor causes regime changes in growth regimes. Currently, the economies of industrialized countries are basically constrained by demand. If the productivity regime stops functioning, the labor supply may emerge as a constraining factor in the long run. On the other hand, the supply of environmental resources is gradually emerging as a fundamental constraint, though the timing and speed of its full-scale appearance is unclear. These factors may constitute a long-term trend of regime changes.

The long-term synthetic effect of environmental measures on the growth regime will appear in various changing shapes over time, through the combination of multiple effects on the productivity and demand regimes, and through interactions with converting growth regimes.

Since this complexity cannot easily be resolved, let us descriptively simulate two contrasting scenarios, from among a wide range of possibilities, in order to gain some insights into possible futures. Let us consider the following scenarios, one in which supply constraints on environmental resources emerge earlier than do constraints on the labor supply, and the other following the opposite order.

Scenario of Environmental Constraints Strengthened environmental measures increase demand and production through the paradox of costs, which raise labor productivity through an increasing return to scale. They also contribute to improved productivity in agriculture, forestry, fishery, tourism and other sectors using the natural environment in the mid- to long-term. Thus, they do not tighten supply constraints on labor. Gradually, the supply constraints on environmental resources become apparent as natural resources are exhausted and international regulations on emissions are intensified. These constraints finally come to determine production activities. Then, as resource productivity has been improved and the natural capital has been enhanced, thanks to environmental measures taken so far, the level of production is relatively high, compared to the case without strengthened environmental measures.

Scenario of Labor Constraints Strengthened environmental measures, while improving resource productivity, lower labor productivity. This is because their effect of increasing demand and production does not significantly work, and the natural capital maintained does not visibly contribute to production. Though the economy has gone beyond the capacity of the earth's ecosystem, supply constraints on environmental resources emerge only slowly because the damages are transferred to specific regions or future generations (i.e., spatial and temporal gaps). In economies with aging and decreasing populations, the constraints on the labor supply become evident first, and come to determine production activities. Due to lowered labor productivity, the level of production at that stage is lower compared to the case without environmental measures. (It should be noted that still, in this case, the constraints on environmental resources will come forth at a later stage, and the level of production at that time may be higher compared to the case without environmental measures.)

These are only a few examples of possible scenarios. The scenarios should depend on the relative strength of multiple effects in specific economies, as well as on the timing and severity of the emergence of environmental constraints.

In resource-importing countries constrained by demand, it is probable, as described above, that environmental measures would contribute to growth, and could lead to higher labor productivity through induced innovations and enlarged working opportunities. In countries with productive and/or beautiful natural environments, and thus with a high potential for agriculture, forestry, tourism, and other industries to make use of them, environmental measures can contribute to higher labor productivity. In countries or areas meeting these conditions, the reality would likely be closer to the scenario of environmental constraints than to that of labor constraints. On the other hand, in countries where supply constraints on labor or capital are already affecting the economy, the probable scenario would be the converse.

5.4 Concluding Remarks

This chapter analyzed the mechanisms of institutional coordination between economy and the environment (i.e., the economy-environment nexus) as well as its interactions with the growth regime, while recognizing this coordination as one of the institutional forms of the *régulation* theory.

When economic growth degrades the environment, actors in society, such as people suffering from the degradation, demand countermeasures of the economy. This feedback from the environment through society to the economy is the driving force of coordination. When there are gaps between relevant actors, such as polluters, victims, etc.—as well as between the actors and the places in which institutions are formed—these feedback loops are not connected. This results in delayed institutional coordination, a phenomenon we refer to as "spatial and temporal gaps of coordination." This is a fundamental problem we are facing in global environmental issues.

The economy functions under coordination by institutions. When the economy faces crises, these institutions are reconsidered and changed. Today's crisis of the earth's ecosystem should be recognized as the most severe structural crisis, which has been endogenously generated by the past growth regime. Large-scale changes in institutions will be required from now on. Institutions in a given domain are required to be compatible with the growth regime, as well as with institutions in other domains. Both environmental and labor institutions have recently been required to prove their compatibility with the competition-oriented international regime.

We have also analyzed, here, the interaction between the economy-environment nexus and the growth regime. First, we analyzed the impacts of the growth regime on the economy-environment nexus, showing that the nature of the Fordist growth regime, also called "intensive accumulation," is one of extensive expansion in the environmental aspect, and thus involves an endogenous mechanism leading to a structural crisis.

Next, we analyzed the effects of the economy-environment nexus on the growth regime in detail, specifying multiple routes through which the cost of environmental measures impacts the demand and productivity regimes.

In a demand regime, an increase in the cost of environmental measures may raise demand by reducing resource importation, increasing labor wages to produce ESGSs, inducing environmental investment, and improving export competitiveness. This means that environmental measures, though adding to costs of production activities, can also raise profits and thus contribute to the growth of the economy as a whole. We call this phenomenon the "paradox of costs for environmental measures." This explains the mechanism of Green Growth.

In a productivity regime, an increase in the cost of environmental measures lowers labor productivity as its direct effect. However, the above-mentioned effect of increasing demand leads to higher productivity since improved economic performance induces innovation. On the other hand, environmental degradations will sooner or later emerge as the fundamental supply constraint. Taking these factors into account, we also discussed the longer-term relationships amongst them.

The structure and status of a given economy will determine how these multiple effects, when combined, impact it. In Chap. 6, we will build a variant of the Kaleckian model in order to analyze more clearly the synthetic effect, in particular, on the demand regime.

References

Aglietta M (1976) Régulation et Crises du Capitalisme: L'expérience des Etats-Unis. Calmann-Lévy, Paris

Amable B (2003) The diversity of modern capitalism. Oxford University Press, Oxford

Aoki M (1996) Toward a comparative institutional analysis. Jpn Econ Rev 47(1):1–19

Becker J, Raza W (1999) Theory of régulation and political ecology: an inevitable separation? Ambiente & Sociedade 5:5–20

Boyer R (1986) La Théorie de la Régulation: Une analyse critique. La Découverte, Paris. English edition: Boyer R (1990) The regulation school: a critical introduction (trans: Charney C). Columbia University Press, New York

Boyer R (2000) The political in the era of globalization and finance: focus on some régulation school research. Int J Urban Reg Res 24(2):274–322

Boyer R (2004) Une théorie du capitalisme est-elle possible? Odile Jacob, Paris

Boyer R (2005) Coherence, diversity, and the evolution of capitalisms: the institutional complementarity hypothesis. EIER 2(1):43–80

Funabashi H (1998) Future of the environmental problems and social change (in Japanese). In: Funabashi H, Iijima N (eds) Lectures on sociology 12: environment. Tokyo University Press, Tokyo, pp 191–224
Jessop B (2002) The future of the capitalist state. Polity Press, Camgridge
Rowthorn R (1982) Demand, real wages and economic growth. Sutudi Economici 18:3–53
Yamada T (1991) Régulation approach (in Japanese). Fujiwara-shoten, Tokyo

Chapter 6
A Kaleckian Model for Economy-Environment Analysis

In this chapter, we build a model to analyze the economic impact of environmental measures. Environmental measures impact economic growth through multiple routes as described in Sect. 5.3.2. We aim to more clearly express them and thus the relationship between the economy-environment nexus and the growth regime (particularly the demand regime). As a method to achieve this, we will develop a variant of the Kaleckian model.

The Kaleckian model originated with Michal Kalecki, who discovered the principle of effective demand simultaneously with, yet separately from, Keynes. Kalecki's approach to effective demand was considered superior in some ways to Keynes's, by Robinson and Kaldor (Robinson 1972; Lavoie 2004). Kalecki highlighted the fact that prices are set by mark-up in oligopolistic economies and that production can be increased with a constant unit cost unless it is under full capacity utilization. Growth models were developed incorporating these points, and have been improved upon since. The Kaleckian model is flexible and provides a common basis for post-Keynesian, structuralism, *régulation*, and other heterodox schools of economic thought (Lavoie 2004). The paradox of costs, in which increasing production costs may raise profit rates, was also presented by using this model (Rowthorn 1982).

A variant of the Kaleckian model for analyzing economy and the environment can be developed by incorporating environmental costs, on the basis of the equation of distribution in Chap. 4.[1]

In the real world, we face contradicting views on environmental measures: growing concerns about expanding costs and emerging expectations for new areas of growth. By analyzing the paradox of costs for environmental measures,

---

[1]This approach of integrating distribution equation and Kaleckian growth model is based on the recognition that changes in distribution affect the amount of surplus itself, and thus the surplus approach of the classical tradition and the effective-demand principle of the Keynesian and Kaleckian tradition can be integrated (Bortis 1996; Uemura 2007).

K. Okuma, *The Evolving Relationship between Economy and Environment*, Evolutionary Economics and Social Complexity Science 8,
DOI 10.1007/978-981-10-4100-6_6

we will untangle them and analyze the possibilities of and conditions for Green Growth.[2]

6.1 The Basic Model Incorporating Environmental Costs

Referring to Lavoie (1992, 2010) and Blecker (2002), we can present a basic Kaleckian model for a closed economy in the following three equations:

$$r = \pi u v \tag{6.1}$$

$$g^s = s_r r \tag{6.2}$$

$$g^i = \gamma_0 + \gamma_u u + \gamma_r \pi v \tag{6.3}$$

where r is profit rate; π is profit share; u is the rate of capacity utilization; v is potential output–capital ratio; g^s is savings and g^i is investment, both normalized by capital stock; and s_r is the propensity to save out of profit. Saving from wages is assumed away. Investment is assumed to depend on the rate of capacity utilization (u) and the full-capacity profit rate (πv), following a specification by Blecker (2002), which is in line with the argument of Marglin and Bhaduri (1990).

The rate of capacity utilization (u) and profit rate (r) are determined by these three equations together with a saving–investment equilibrium condition ($g^i = g^s$). The impacts of change in profit share (π) on them are analyzed by comparative statics in relation to state of the economy, represented by parameters of s_r, γ_0, γ_u, and γ_r. In addition, because of $g^i = s_r r$ (the Cambridge equation) from Eq. 6.2 and the saving–investment equilibrium condition, meaning that profit rate is directly connected to accumulation rate, the impacts on accumulation rate (g^i) are simultaneously analyzed.

By incorporating environmental elements into this model, we build a model that can analyze the impacts of a change in the share of environmental-measure costs on the level of capacity utilization (u) and profit rate (r).

First, we specify environmental costs as additional elements of production costs and distribution in Eq. 6.1.[3] We have presented rent and environmental-measure

[2]We use a Kaleckian model because of our emphasis on the relation between costs of environmental measures and demand. There can be other approaches on the common basis of *régulation* theory or post-Keynesian theory. For example, Uni (2011) took steps to apply the cumulative causation model as in Boyer (1988) to environmental issues by estimating the "productivity regime in a broader sense" and considering its institutional implications.

[3]Although the current size of environmental elements in distribution is far smaller than wage and profit, a study has indicated that the costs of additional countermeasures against global warming will go beyond 2% of the GDP in Japan's case (Central Environment Policy Council 2010). This size together with the speed of change indicates the possible impact on the economy, which justifies this way of modeling as one of the possible approaches.

cost as elements of the equation of distribution, based on the concept of three-dimensional distributions (see Chap. 4), which is reprinted here as follows:

$$1 = r/uv_p + w/p\lambda_p + (\rho + \rho_e)/p\varepsilon_p \tag{4.7}$$

where $v_p = \bar{Y}/K_p$ is the ratio of potential output to production capital, $\lambda_p = Y/L_p$ is production-labor productivity, $\varepsilon_p = Y/N_p$ is production-resources productivity, ρ is money rent rate, and $\rho_e = p_e E/N_p$ is the cost of environmental measures per unit consumption of production resources; while Y is output; E is consumption of environmental-resources-substituting goods and services (ESGSs); and K_p, L_p, and N_p are capital stock, labor input, and consumption of natural resources, used for production other than ESGSs (see Chap. 4 for further notation on symbols).

Using this equation, we change Eq. 6.1 into

$$r = (1 - W_s - R_s - e)uv_p \tag{6.1.1}$$

where $W_s = w/p\lambda_p$ is the share of wages for production labor, $R_s = \rho/p\varepsilon_p$ is the share of rent for production resources, and $e = \rho_e/p\varepsilon_p = p_e E/pY$ is the share of the cost of environmental measures.

Here, a change in e may affect R_s and W_s. As explained in Chap. 4, an increase in e improves ε_p, leading to a reduction in R_s, thus R_s is written in linear form as

$$R_s = R_{s0} - \phi e \tag{6.4}$$

where ϕ is the rate of induced reduction in rent to the cost of environmental measures, or the recovery rate of environmental-measure cost.[4] Assuming that additional environmental measures save some resource costs but do not pay by themselves, we obtain $\phi \in (0, 1)$.

An increase in e, which is partly recovered by a reduction in R_s, reduces π without affecting W_s in quantitative adjustments, while it reduces real wage rate and W_s in price adjustments. This varied effect can be written as

$$W_s = W_{s0} - \theta(1 - \phi)e \tag{6.5}$$

where $\theta \in (0, 1)$ is the share of environmental-measure cost borne by wages. We understand that θ reflects the bargaining powers of capitalists and workers.[5] We note that, empirically, θ could be assumed to be null for the short to midterm when simplicity is needed.[6]

[4]Though strictly this relation is not linear in view of increasing marginal costs, linear expression can be employed for simplicity in this model designed to analyze the impacts of marginal change in e.

[5]This way of formulation is in line with models of conflict theory of inflation (e.g., Cassetti 2003).

[6]Pollution-prevention expenditures in Japanese enterprises in the 1970s were covered by a reduction of profits and other cost cuts rather than raising prices (Environment Agency 1992).

Substituting (6.4) and (6.5) into (6.1.1), we have

$$r = [\pi_0 - (1 - \theta)(1 - \phi)e]uv_p \tag{6.1.2}$$

where $\pi_0 = 1 - W_{s0} - R_{s0}$ is a constant in relation to e. $[\pi_0 - (1 - \theta)(1 - \phi)e]$ represents share of profit for production capital and is hereafter written as π_p.

When taking into account savings from rent, saving is written as

$$S = s_r rpK + s_\rho \rho N \tag{6.2.1}$$

where S is gross savings, rpK is gross profits, ρN is rents, and s_ρ is propensity to save from rents.

Normalizing this equation by capital stock while assuming that production factors are utilized in the same proportion between the ESGS sector and the production sector, we obtain[7]

$$g^s = s_r r + s_\rho R_s uv_p. \tag{6.2.2}$$

Investment is influenced by capacity utilization and profit rate, as in Eq. 6.3. In addition, when focusing on environmental measures, investment is induced by a growing demand for ESGSs, as was presented as the fourth effect in Sect. 5.3.2. This effect is related to the structural change in industry, which is distinct from the effect of overall effective demand, as reflected in capacity utilization. However, this cannot readily be dealt with by simple comparative statics, due to its dynamic nature. At this stage, we represent this effect by a constant and change Eq. 6.3 into

$$g^i = \gamma_0 + \gamma_u u + \gamma_r \pi_p v_p + \gamma_{0e} \tag{6.3.1}$$

where γ_{0e} is a constant representing investment induced by increasing consumption of ESGSs. Further consideration will be given to this in Sect. 6.3.

By solving Eqs. 6.1.2, 6.2.2, and 6.3.1 under saving–investment equilibrium conditions, levels of u and r are determined. By comparative statics, the effects of change in e on them can be analyzed in relation to conditions of the economy represented in parameters s_r, s_ρ, γ_0, γ_u, and γ_r, as well as the nature of environmental measures represented in ϕ.

Skipping the detailed analysis of this model, we go on to consider a model that can be used to analyze resource-importing countries.

[7]Rent normalized by capital stock are transformed as follows: $R/pK = \rho N/pK = \rho N_p/pK_p = R_s pY/pK_p = R_s uv_p$

6.2 The Model of a Resource-Importing Country

Incorporating imports, according to the structure in Table 4.1 in Chap. 4, we change Eq. 6.1.1 into

$$r = (1 - M_s - W_s - R_s - e)uv_p \tag{6.1.3}$$

where $M_s = pM_p/pY$ is the share of imports used for production, excluding the rent equivalent; and R_s is the share of rents for production resources, including hereafter the rent equivalent as $R_s = \rho(N_d + N_m)/pY$ (see Table 4.1 in Chap. 4 for further information on symbols). Because an increase in E does not directly increase Y, M_s is constant in relation to e. Thus, Eq. 6.1.2 is maintained with a revised notation: $\pi_0 = 1 - W_{s0} - R_{s0} - M_s$ is a constant in relation to e.

If we assume all natural resources without public goods are imported, no rents are saved within the country and the saving function goes back to Eq. 6.2.

Formulation of trade has a wide range of possibilities. Here we take simple linear equations of imports and exports: the former includes the share of environmental-measure cost as well as capacity utilization rate as explicit variables, while the latter includes profit share as one explicit variable and includes other factors (such as exchange rate and scale of world trade) in the constant terms. At this stage we also represent, by a constant, the effect of environmental measures on accelerating innovations and improving export competitiveness, which was presented as the fifth effect in Sect. 5.3.2, since it cannot readily be dealt with by simple comparative statics due to its dynamic nature. Thus we obtain

$$m = m_0 + m_u u - m_e e \tag{6.6}$$

$$x = x_0 + x_\pi \pi + x_{0e} \tag{6.7}$$

where m is imports and x is exports, both normalized by capital stock. x_{0e} is a constant representing the effect of environmental measures on improving export competitiveness (further consideration will be given to this topic in the next section). The sign of m_u is positive, since the rise in capacity utilization increases imports. m_e is assumed to be positive, since environmental measures improve resource efficiency and reduce rent that otherwise would leak abroad. x_π is assumed to be positive as high profit share means moderate wages and other production costs, implying high price competitiveness. For entirely resource-importing countries, the relation $m_e = \phi uv_p$ exists because a change in rent by resource savings corresponds to a change in imports. Parameters m_e together with ϕ represent the first effect of the cost of environmental measures on the demand regime, as raised in Sect. 5.3.2.

The saving–investment equilibrium condition in this open economy is[8]

[8]This model abstracts from government deficit, which could be added to the right side for a more precise presentation of the saving–investment balance, on the assumption that it is not determined by a function of variables such as e, u, and r, but by policy factors.

$$g^s = g^i + x - m. \tag{6.8}$$

Combining Eqs. 6.1.2, 6.2, 6.3.1, 6.6, 6.7, and 6.8, levels of u and r in the equilibrium are determined. By comparative statics, we can analyze the effect of a change in e on them, in relation to conditions of the economy represented in parameters s_r, γ_0, γ_u, γ_r, m_0, m_u, x_0 and x_π as well as the nature of environmental measures represented in ϕ and m_e.[9]

Equation 6.1.2 represents what Lavoie (1992) called the price–cost curve (PC curve) by using a graphical presentation in the u-r plane (Fig. 6.1). A rise in e reduces the slope and thus shifts the curve downward.

Then, substituting Eqs. 6.2, 6.3.1, 6.6, and 6.7 into 6.8, we have

$$r = \frac{\gamma_u - m_u}{s_r} u + \frac{-(\gamma_r v_p + x_\pi)(1-\theta)(1-\phi)e + m_e e + \gamma_{0e} + x_{0e} + c}{s_r} \tag{6.9}$$

where $c = \gamma_0 + x_0 - m_0 + \gamma_r \pi_0 v_p$ is a constant in relation to e.

This represents what Lavoie (1992) called the effective-demand curve (ED curve) (Fig. 6.1). The slope of the ED curve is smaller than that of the PC curve on the assumption of the Keynesian stability condition (Lavoie 1992).[10] Moreover, it is positive, if assuming a closed economy as in the canonical Kaleckian model (Fig. 6.1), but can possibly be negative in this model incorporating trades if sensitivity of import to capacity utilization is high (i.e., m_u is large) (Fig. 6.2). The intercept is assumed to be positive so that the model has a solution.

A rise in e induces two different effects on the ED curve. First, it lowers the intercept through reduction in investment and exports represented in $[-(\gamma_r v_p + x_\pi)(1-\theta)(1-\phi)e]$, which is the common effect with other costs such as wages. Second, it increases the intercept through reduction in imports of environmental resources represented in $m_e e$. In addition, if it increases γ_{0e} or x_{0e}, though these are presented as constants here, the intercept should further rise. Consequently, the ED curve may shift either downward or upward.

The equilibrium rate of capacity utilization (u^*) and that of profit (r^*) are determined at the intersection of the PC curve and the ED curve. Without the second effect on the ED curve, the costs of environmental measures have basically the same effects as wages in the usual Kaleckian models. A rise in e may either increase or decrease u and r, depending on the slope and the shift of the curves, which is illustrated as a move from A to B in Figs. 6.1 and 6.2. This is the second effect in Sect. 5.3.2. When u and r increase, it corresponds to the "paradox of costs"

[9]In this model with import, $g^i = g^s$ does not hold and g^i is not directly linked to r, which precludes the simple analysis of the accumulation rate as in the basic model in the previous section. It is a remaining issue to be studied, to develop methods that clearly present impacts on the accumulation rate.

[10]Keynesian stability condition, meaning that a rise in capacity utilization reduces excessive demand, is presented as $[\, s_r \pi_p v_p - (\gamma_u - m_u) > 0]$ in this model.

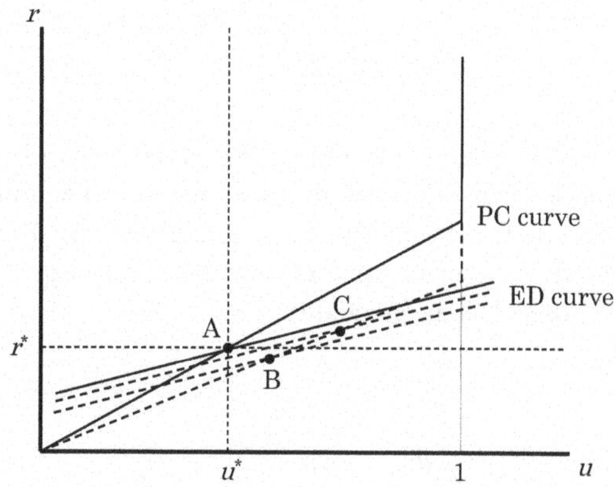

Fig. 6.1 Graphical presentation of the model (Reproduced from Okuma 2012)

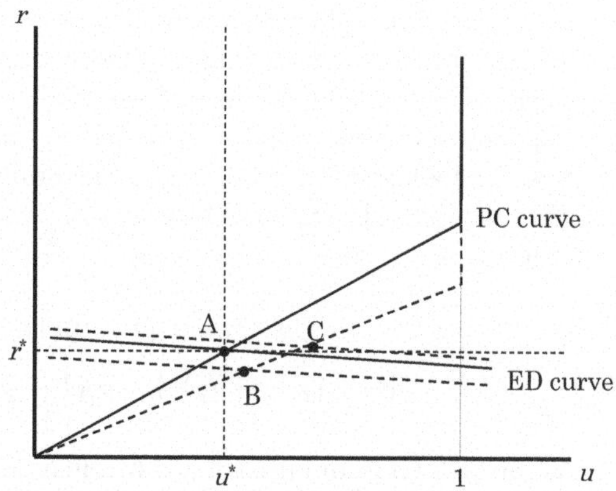

Fig. 6.2 Graphical presentation of the model (with ED curve of negative slope)

a la Rowthorn (1982) and to the "cooperative stagnationist" regime under a recent Kaleckian categorization (Blecker 2002). On the other hand, when u increases but r falls, it corresponds to the "conflictive stagnationist" regime (ibid.)

When taking into consideration the second effect on the ED curve, a rise in e increases $m_e e$, which brings the ED curve upward. This is illustrated as a move to C in Figs. 6.1 and 6.2. This increases the possibility that the rise in e increases r even when the ordinary "paradox of costs" does not work. This is a formal presentation of the "paradox of costs for environmental measures" introduced in Sect. 5.3.2, representing the aggregate effect of the first and second effects in that section.

Referring to the methodology in Lavoie (1992), let us specify the conditions for e to increase u and r.[11] At first, we look at the effect on u. By partially differentiating the PC function Eq. 6.1.2 and ED function Eq. 6.9 for e, we have

[11]We use here a method for analysis using graphical presentations, which is one of the Kaleckian traditions, in view of applying it to the analysis of dynamic effects in Sect. 6.3. One can obtain the same results by applying a method that uses total differentials.

$$\partial r^{\mathrm{PC}}/\partial e = -(1-\theta)\ (1-\phi)uv_p \tag{6.10}$$

$$\partial r^{\mathrm{ED}}/\partial e = \left[-\left(\gamma_r v_p + x_\pi\right)(1-\theta)(1-\phi) + m_e\right]/s_r. \tag{6.11}$$

As can be seen from Figs. 6.1 and 6.2, in order for u to increase as e rises, the ED curve needs to shift more in the positive direction (i.e., less in the negative direction) than the PC curve at a given initial rate of u when the slope of the ED curve is either positive or negative. From Eqs. 6.10 and 6.11, these conditions are expressed as an inequality:

$$F_u(1-\phi) + m_e > 0 \tag{6.12}$$

where $F_u = (s_r uv_p - \gamma_r v_p - x_\pi)(1-\theta)$.

F_u represents the effect of increasing costs influencing on the saving–investment balance through distribution, which is common to various costs. $(1-\phi)$ and m_e represent the effects of environmental measures reducing rent and imports through saving resources, which are unique to the environmental-measure cost. The former corresponds to the second effect, that is, the "cost-demand effect," and the latter corresponds to the first effect, that is, the "resource-saving effect" in Sect. 5.3.2.

Next, we look at the effect on r. By transforming the PC function in Eq. 6.1.2 and the ED function in Eq. 6.9 into functions of r and partially differentiating them for e, we have

$$\partial u^{\mathrm{PC}}/\partial e = (1-\theta)(1-\phi)r/v_p{\pi_p}^2 \tag{6.13}$$

$$\partial u^{\mathrm{ED}}/\partial e = \left[\left(\gamma_r v_p + x_\pi\right)(1-\theta)(1-\phi) - m_e\right]/(\gamma_u - m_u) \tag{6.14}$$

As can be seen from Figs. 6.1 and 6.2, in order for r to increase as e rises, the PC curve needs to shift more in the positive direction than the ED curve at a given initial rate of r when the slope of the ED curve is positive (Fig. 6.1). It needs to shift less when the slope is negative (Fig. 6.2). These conditions are expressed as an inequality:

$$F_r(1-\phi) + m_e > 0 \tag{6.15}$$

where $F_r = [(\gamma_u - m_u)u/\pi_p - (\gamma_r v_p + x_\pi)](1-\theta)$.

F_r, in the same way as F_u, represents the effect corresponding to the "cost-demand effect," which is common to various costs. $(1-\phi)$ and m_e represent the effects corresponding to the "resource-saving effect," which is unique to environmental measures. This condition will be met either when the value of F_r is positive or when the left side of the inequality is made positive by ϕ and m_e (even when F_r is negative). The former corresponds to the ordinary "paradox of costs" and the latter to the "paradox of costs for environmental measures."

The value of F_r depends on the values of $(\gamma_u - m_u)$ and $(\gamma_r v_p + x_\pi)$. The former can be understood as the "accelerator effect" (i.e., an increase in investment leads to a rise in capacity utilization rate, which induces further investments) minus the "leakage effect" (i.e., a higher capacity utilization rate leads to more imports, which reduce demand). The letter can be understood as the effect in which an increase in costs (appearing as a fall in profit share) reduces investment and export.

For example, when there is a significant accelerator effect in a relatively closed economy, the condition is met even when environmental measures have no resource-saving effect. On the other hand, when investment responds strongly to the profit rate under financial constraints, and trade is highly sensitive to prices and business cycles in the globalized economy, environmental measures need to have larger resource-saving effects if profit rate is to increase.

In the case of entirely resource-importing countries, under the assumption of $\phi \in (0, 1)$, Eq. 6.15 can be transformed into

$$\phi/(1-\phi) > -F_r/uv_p. \tag{6.16}$$

Using this inequality, we can estimate what types of environmental measures, in terms of recovery rate of costs (ϕ), should have the effect of raising the profit rate under given economic conditions represented by parameters such as γ_u, γ_r, m_u, and x_π.

The model presented above enables the analysis of the "paradox of costs for environmental measures" for resource-importing countries. A summary of the model is presented in Table 6.1.

Table 6.1 Summary of the model

a. Main equations		
Profit rate	$r=[\pi_0-(1-\theta)(1-\phi)e]uv_p$	(6.1.2)
Savings	$g^s=s_r r$	(6.2)
Investment	$g^i=\gamma_0+\gamma_u u+\gamma_r\pi_p v_p+\gamma_{0e}$	(6.3.1)
Imports	$m=m_0+m_u u-m_e e$	(6.6)
Exports	$x=x_0+x_\pi\pi_p+x_{0e}$	(6.7)
I-S equilibrium	$g^s=g^i+x-m$	(6.8)
b. Analyzing impacts of environmental-measure cost		
(a) Condition for capacity utilization rate to rise		
$F_u(1-\phi)+m_e>0$ where $F_u=(s_r uv_p-\gamma_r v_p-x_\pi)\ (1-\theta)$		(6.12)
(b) Condition for profit rate to rise (paradox of costs)		
$F_r(1-\phi)+m_e>0$ where $F_r=[(\gamma_u-m_u)u/\pi_p-(\gamma_r v_p+x_\pi)](1-\theta)$		(6.15)
(c) Inequality to calculate minimum recovery rate of EMC that raise profit rate		
$\phi/(1-\phi)>-F_r/uv_p$		(6.16)

Notes: e is environmental-measure cost (EMC) share; θ is the share of EMC borne by wage; ϕ is recovery rate of EMC; u is capacity utilization rate; v_p is potential-output to production-capital rate; π_p is profit share for production capital

6.3 Analyzing Dynamic Effects

Among the multiple effects of environmental measures on the demand regime, discussed in Sect. 5.3.2, the model above only presents as constant terms the fourth ("investment-inducing") effect and the fifth ("export competitiveness") effect, because they cannot be readily analyzed by simple comparative statics due to their dynamic nature. However, these effects are widely recognized as historically observed facts and are often mentioned in discussions on Green Growth and other related themes. Thus, we attempt to formalize these effects and analyze their implications not by simple comparative statics, but on the basis of graphical expressions.

First, we formalize the investment-inducing effect, which was represented by a constant γ_{0e} in the investment function Eq. 6.3.1. This is the effect in which growing environmental measures induce the investment necessary to implement them. This was historically observed, for example, as a significant increase in pollution abatement investments under the rapidly strengthened pollution control in the 1970s in Japan.[12] By focusing on the growth of environmental measures, γ_{0e} can be formalized as

$$\gamma_{0e} = \gamma_e \Delta E / K \tag{6.17}$$

where $\Delta E = E_t - E_{t-1}$ is the growth of environmental-measure cost (E). $\Delta E/K$ is positive while E is increasing, but becomes zero when E becomes stable. Thus, $\gamma_e \Delta E/K$ is a short-term effect that works immediately but does not last long.[13]

Second, we formalize the export competitiveness effect which was represented by a constant x_{0e} in the export function Eq. 6.7. This is the effect of strengthened export competitiveness because of environmental technologies. Though there are various factors in technological development, we focus on the factor of "learning by doing" from the viewpoint of analyzing the effect of environmental measures. This was also historically observed, for example, as an established recognition that the Japanese automobile industry improved its technological capacities by struggling to meet the strict regulatory standards of the 1970s–1980s (OECD 1991; Environment Agency 1992). By focusing on accumulated experiences of environmental measures, x_{0e} can be formalized as

[12]In Japan, total private investment was generally constant during the 1970s in spite of the oil crisis. In this period, pollution abatement investments expanded and their ratio to total investments soared to nearly 20% around 1975, which should have supported the level of total investment. A macro-econometric model study estimated that the antipollution measures induced a 7.4% increase in total private investments in 1975 (Environment Agency 1992).

[13]Since consumption of ESGSs has a tendency to grow, as discussed in Chap. 3, we can assume $\Delta E/K$ as positive in general.

$$x_{0e} = x_e T/K \tag{6.18}$$

where T is the accumulation of experiences of environmental measures. By taking into account methodologies for estimating R&D stocks by the perpetual inventory method, one possible way of formulation is $[T_t = E_t + (1-\delta)T_{t-1}]$, where δ is the depreciation rate of technological knowledge. When E increases, T reaches a high after a certain period of time. Thus, $x_e T/K$ is considered an effect of mid- to long-term nature.

These are effects of dynamic nature and cannot be readily analyzed by simple comparative statics. However, in the graphical presentation in Figs. 6.1 and 6.2, they can be presented as changes in the intercept shifting the ED curve, on which basis we can analyze their impacts. By incorporating the formalization of γ_{0e} and x_{0e} (i.e., Eqs. 6.17 and 6.18) above, Eq. 6.9 representing the ED curve is changed into

$$r = \frac{\gamma_u - m_u}{s_r} u + \frac{-(\gamma_r v_p + x_\pi)(1-\theta)(1-\phi)e + m_e e + \gamma_e \Delta E/K + x_e T/K + c}{s_r}. \tag{6.9.1}$$

Let us consider a method to evaluate how these effects impact u and r. Their impacts depend on the timing and the magnitude of a shift in the ED curve. The magnitude of the shift of the curve at each term is indicated by the values of $\gamma_e \Delta E/K$ and $x_e T/K$, which can be calculated by using actual values in the analysis of the past. Since $\gamma_e \Delta E/K$ and $x_e T/K$ are located in the same position with $m_e e$ in Eq. 6.9.1, $(\gamma_e \Delta E/K + x_e T/K)$ is comparable with $m_e e$ in terms of the magnitude of its shift. Therefore, as long as we interpret with caution, bearing in mind fluctuations over terms, their impacts can be evaluated by adding $[(\gamma_e \Delta E/K + x_e T/K)/e]$ to m_e in inequalities 6.12 and 6.15.

Multiple effects and their relations to the "paradox of costs for environmental measures" discussed above can be summarized in Fig. 6.3.

The above model helps us to understand more clearly the structure and relationships of multiple effects of environmental measures on economic growth. It also opens up the possibility for quantitative estimations in the empirical analysis of specific economies. We conduct an econometric analysis on the Japanese experience in Chap. 8.

It should be noted that the analysis above is basically on the state of an economy with remaining capacity of production, where demand determines the production. If the economy has reached its limits of capacity, where $u = 1$, the effects of costs to raise u cannot work. In this context, one may recall that neoclassical economists recognize long-term production to be determined only by supply capacity, and not influenced by demand. However, many researchers of Kaleckian consider that this model applies also to the long term, based on the recognition that the higher performance of the economy enhances supply capacity in the long term, through a possible

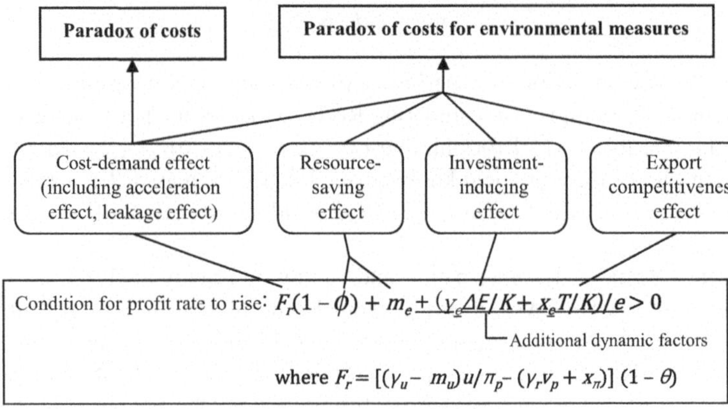

Fig. 6.3 Multiple effects of environmental measures and paradox of costs

increase in labor supply due to higher labor force participation (especially by women) or immigration, as well as through technological progress by the learning-by-doing effect or through faster dissemination of innovations (Lavoie 2004).

6.4 Concluding Remarks

In this chapter, we developed a model for analyzing the impact of environmental measures on economic growth by incorporating environmental costs into the Kaleckian model. The model is composed of equations explaining profit rate, savings, investment, and import and export, by using variables such as capacity utilization rate, profit share, and environmental-measure cost. By analyzing this model with a focus on changes in capacity utilization and profit rate, it was shown that an increase in environmental-measure cost can lead to higher capacity utilization and profit rates under certain conditions.

Strengthened environmental measures, while raising production costs, alter the I-S balance and raise capacity utilization. Thus, they may raise profit rates when investment is sensitive to capacity utilization (i.e., the "acceleration effect" is large) and importation is not so sensitive to it (i.e., the "leakage effect" is small). Moreover, environmental measures have the effect of reducing imports of natural resources, inducing investment in environmental equipment and facilities in the short term, and strengthening export competitiveness by encouraging innovations in the mid to long term. These combined effects enlarge the possibility of raising capacity utilization and profit rates.

We presented these effects in the model and identified conditions for them to raise profit rates, which formally explains the mechanism and conditions of the "paradox of costs for environmental measures" as well as Green Growth.

This model can be applied to econometric analyses. In Chap. 8, we will apply it to Japanese experiences in order to clarify what effects pollution abatement policies in the 1970s had on the economy and what effects may possibly appear if environmental measures are strengthened now.

The theoretical considerations above, in Chaps. 3, 4, 5, and 6, provided us with tools for the analysis. In Part III, let us proceed with the empirical analysis of Japan's experience from the postwar era to today, in order to understand how the relationship between economy and the environment has evolved and to search for insights into the future.

References

Blecker RA (2002) Distribution, demand and growth in neo-Kaleckian macro models. In: Setterfield M (ed) The economics of demand-led growth: challenging the supply-side vision of the long run. Edward Elgar, Northampton, pp 129–152

Bortis H (1996) Notes on the surplus approach in political economy. In: Arestis P, Palma G, Sawyer M (eds) Capital controversy, post-Keynesian economics and the history of economic thought. Routledge, London, pp 11–23

Boyer R (1988) Formalizing growth regimes. In: Dosi G, Christopher F et al (eds) Technical change and economic theory. Printer Publishers, London, pp 608–630

Cassetti M (2003) Bargaining power, effective demand and technical progress: a Kaleckian model of growth. Camb J Econ 27:449–464

Central Environment Policy Council (2010) Interim report on vision of policies and measures to achieve the mid- to long-term emission reduction targets (in Japanese). http://www.env.go.jp/council/06earth/y0611-19.html. Accessed 25 Nov 2016

Environment Agency (1992) Quality of the environment in Japan, 1992. Environment Agency, Tokyo

Lavoie M (1992) Foundations of post-Keynesian economic analysis. Edward Elgar, Aldershot

Lavoie M (2004) L'économie postkeynésienne. La Découverte, Paris

Lavoie M (2010) Surveying short-run and long-run stability issues with the Kalickian model of growth. In: Setterfield M (ed) Handbook of alternative theories of economic growth. Edward Elger, Northampton, pp 132–156

Marglin SA, Bhaduri A (1990) Profit squeeze and Keynesian theory. In: Marglin SA, Shor JB (eds) The golden age of capitalism. Oxford University Press, Oxford, pp 153–186

OECD (1991) Environmental performance reviews: Japan. OECD, Paris

Okuma K (2012) An analytical framework for the relationship between environmental measures and economic growth based on the régulation theory: key concepts and a simple model. Evol Institut Econ Rev 9(1):141–168

Robinson J (1972) The second crisis of economic theory. Am Econ Rev 62(1):1–10

Rowthorn R (1982) Demand, real wages and economic growth. Sutudi Economici 18:3–54

Uemura H (2007) Reproduction of socio-economic system and inequity in distribution (in Japanese). Polit Econ Q 43(4):5–15

Uni H (2011) Economic growth and greenhouse gas emissions: an analysis using a cumulative causation model. Paper presented at the 23rd Annual Conference of the European Association for Evolutionary Political Economy, Vienna, 27–30 Oct 2011

Part III
Long-Term Transformation in Japan

Chapter 7
Overview of Long-Term Trends of the Economy-Environment Nexus in Japan

In Part III, we will conduct a historical analysis on the relationship between economy and the environment in Japan from the postwar era to today, using the theoretical framework discussed in Part II.

As we saw in Chap. 2, the world economy has been rapidly growing and environmental burdens have also been rapidly increasing since the nineteenth century, under the capitalist and market economy. During this period, the structure generating the growth (the growth regime) has changed over time, as has the relationship between economy and the environment (the economy-environment nexus). This book analyzes the long-term transformation of this relationship by taking Japanese history as an example and focusing on the period from the 1960s to around 2010. Japan has come through contrasting experiences of severe pollution damages in the postwar era of high growth, as well as rapid improvements in resource productivity through pollution abatements and energy savings in the 1970s. It should, therefore, provide us with one of the best examples to analyze transformation in the economy-environment nexus.

As the starting point of this analysis, this chapter takes an overview of how the economy-environment nexus in Japan has changed over time. First, we review the long-term trends of economic growth, environmental burdens, and environmental measures. Second, to analyze the relationship among them, we conduct long-term estimates of environmental costs as quantitative indices reflecting the status of the economy-environment nexus. Third, by using this information, we provide an overview of the development of institutional coordination within the economy-environment nexus.

K. Okuma, *The Evolving Relationship between Economy and Environment*,
Evolutionary Economics and Social Complexity Science 8,
DOI 10.1007/978-981-10-4100-6_7

7.1 Economic Growth, Environmental Burdens, and Environmental Measures

As we saw in Chap. 3, economy and the environment evolve as interacting with one another through a feedback loop that goes through society. To analyze their evolving relationship, the first step should be to trace each phase of this loop: economy, the environment, and society. Let us overview the trends of economic growth (representing the state of the economy), environmental burdens (representing the pressures on the environment), and institutions for countermeasures (representing the reactions from society).

The trend of economic growth is shown in Fig. 7.1. This book analyzes economic growth by focusing on the capital accumulation rate, following the tradition of *régulation* and post-Keynesian theories (sources of data and methods of estimation are shown in the appendix). The accumulation rate changes in a similar trend with the profit rate. Japan's accumulation rate was high in the 1960s but fell around 1970, indicating that the mechanism of the postwar high growth had reached its limit. It again rose and stayed relatively high in the 1980s, reflecting the export-led growth at the time. It fell around 1990, due to the collapse of the bubble, and stayed low for a long time. It again started to rise from around 2000, but fell, around 2008, due to the world financial crisis.

Environmental burdens change as they are impacted by economic growth. Figure 7.2 shows emissions of carbon dioxide (CO_2) and sulfur oxides (SO_x) as representatives of various environmental burdens (sources of data and methods of estimation are shown in the appendix). Both CO_2 and SO_x emissions soared in the 1960s, as the economy grew. After that, SO_x fell in the first half of the 1970s. CO_2, on the other hand, slowed down in the mid-1970s, but continued to stay high until recently.

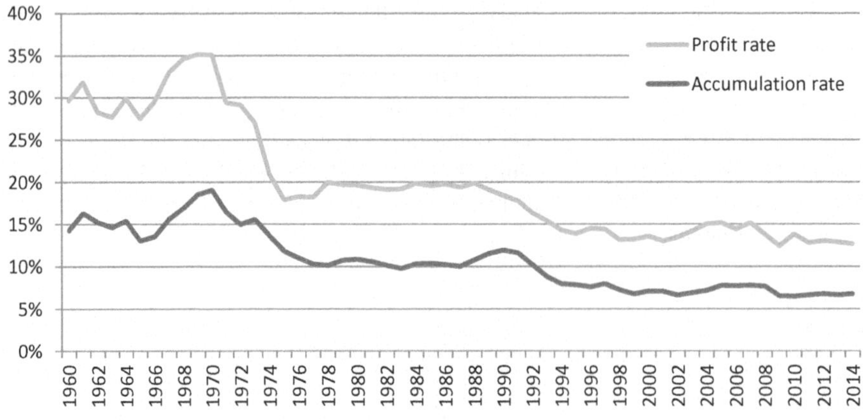

Fig. 7.1 Accumulation rate and profit rate in Japan

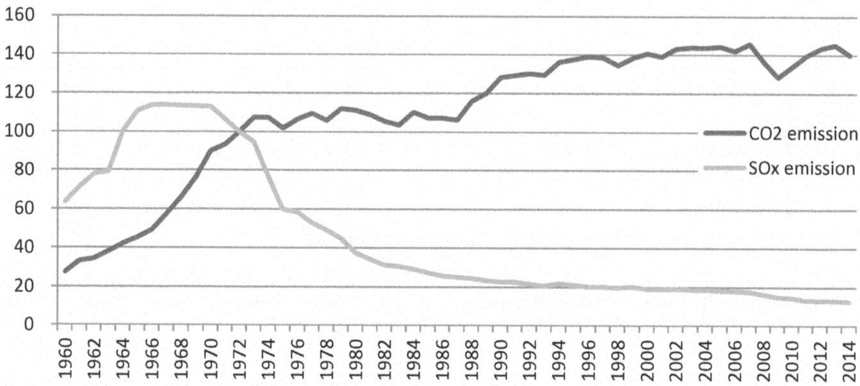

Fig. 7.2 CO_2 emission and SO_x emission in Japan (Index: 100 at 1972)

In response to these environmental burdens and resulting damages, environmental institutions were formulated. The history of the formulation of legislation and other institutions is outlined in Table 7.1. As can be seen from the table, environmental institutions have been formulated with periods of progress and stagnation. From the end of 1960s to the 1970s, regulations and other institutions for pollution abatement were introduced and strengthened. In the 1980s, formulation of institutions was stagnated. From the 1990s onward, institutions in the fields of global warming policy, as well as waste management and recycling policy, have been formulated step by step.

These three factors—economic growth, environmental burdens, and environmental institutions—have interactively evolved, as can be observed in the correlations among these figures and tables above. For example, as a result of the high growth in the postwar era, the emission of pollutants expanded. This caused health damages, which led to the introduction of strict regulations in the 1970s. In turn, these regulations reduced SO_x emission without showing negative impacts on growth. Next, stable growth in the 1980s led to continued large-scale CO_2 emission and other environmental burdens. Institutions related to global warming and recycling were introduced to act against these burdens in the 1990s. More recently, in response to the global financial crisis in 2008, policies to promote environment-friendly automobiles and electric appliances were introduced with twofold purposes: economic stimulus and environmental protection.

To analyze these interactions more clearly, it is beneficial to look at environmental costs as indices reflecting the status of the economy-environment nexus. In the next section, we conduct a long-term estimation of the environmental costs based on the definition and formalization discussed in Chaps. 3 and 4.

Table 7.1 Development of the environmental institutions in Japan (Okuma 2016)

Year	Legislation/Policies
1968	Basic Law for Pollution Control, Air Pollution Prevention Law
1969	
1970	Pollution Session of the Diet (14 bills: Amended Basic Law, Waste Management Law, Water Pollution Control Law, etc.)
1971	Environment Agency established
1972	→ *During the 1970s, regulatory standards continuously tightened*
1973	
1974	Total Emission Control of SO_x
1975	
1976	
1977	
1978	Strict standards on automobile exhaust ("Japanese Muskie Act")
1979	Energy Saving Law
1980	
1981	
1982	
1983	Abolition of Environmental Impact Assessment Bill
1984	
1985	
1986	
1987	
1988	
1989	
1990	Recycled Resources Utilization Law, Amended Waste Control Law
1991	
1992	
1993	Basic Environment Law
1994	
1995	Containers and Packaging Recycling Law
1996	
1997	Environmental Assessment Law, Voluntary Action Plan by industry
1998	Global Warming Mitigation Law, Amended Energy-Saving Law, Electric Appliances Recycling Law
1999	
2000	Basic Act for Sound-Material-Based Society, Green Procurement Law
2001	Ministry of the Environment established
2002	End-of-Life Vehicle Recycling Law, Amended Global Warming Mitigation Law and Energy-Saving Law
2003	
2004	
2005	Amended Global Warming Mitigation Law and Energy-Saving Law
2006	
2007	

(continued)

Table 7.1 (continued)

Year	Legislation/Policies
2008	Amended Global Warming Mitigation Law and Energy-Saving Law
2009	Eco-Car Subsidy Scheme, Eco-Points Scheme for Electric Appliances
2010	
2011	
2012	Carbon Tax, Feed-in Tariff Scheme
2013	Amended Global Warming Mitigation Law and Energy-Saving Law
2014	
2015	
2016	Plan for Global Warming Countermeasures

7.2 Long-Term Estimation of Environmental Costs

To obtain objective indices reflecting the status of coordination in the economy-environment nexus, we conduct a long-term estimation of costs related to the environment, namely, the costs of environmental measures, rents, and latent environmental costs from the 1960s to around 2010 in Japan.

First, we estimate the costs of environmental measures. We do this by calculating the intermediate inputs of environmental-resources-substituting goods and services (ESGSs) of important categories (corresponding to p_eX_{ep} in Sect. 4.2). In so doing, we refer to the methodology used in the Japanese estimation of the System of Environmental-Economic Accounting (SEEA) (Japan Research Institute 2004).[1] As categories of ESGSs, we take up internal pollution control, internal energy-saving, waste management, and environmental research and development. The results, presented as shares in the output, are shown in Fig. 7.3. The data sources and estimation methods are shown in the appendix.

It should be noted that there will still be other categories of environmental-measure costs, though we abstract from them in view of the magnitude as well as the data availability. Intermediate inputs among different ESGS sectors should also be deducted from the total, if we are to estimate the exact value in accordance with the concept of a vertically integrated sector of ESGSs in Table 4.1 in Sect. 4.2, though in this case we assume them away since their amounts are small.

Second, we estimate rents. In the case of resource-importing countries like Japan, most rents are included in importation, and the rent equivalent in importation (corresponding to ρN_m in Sect. 4.2) should be estimated. Although it should be included in various goods and services, this study regards the importation value of natural resources as rent equivalent, in view of its magnitude and of the data availability. The results, presented as shares in the output, are shown in Fig. 7.4.

[1]When compared with the estimation by Japanese Research Institute (2004), this estimation covers a long-term period, omitting some categories of smaller magnitude, while adding energy-saving and environmental R&D in line with our interest in climate change and competitiveness, respectively.

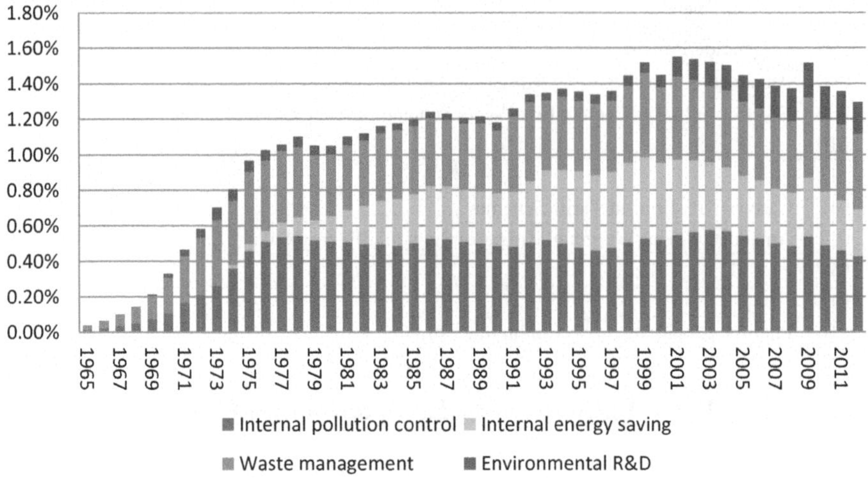

Fig. 7.3 Ratio of environmental-measure costs to output

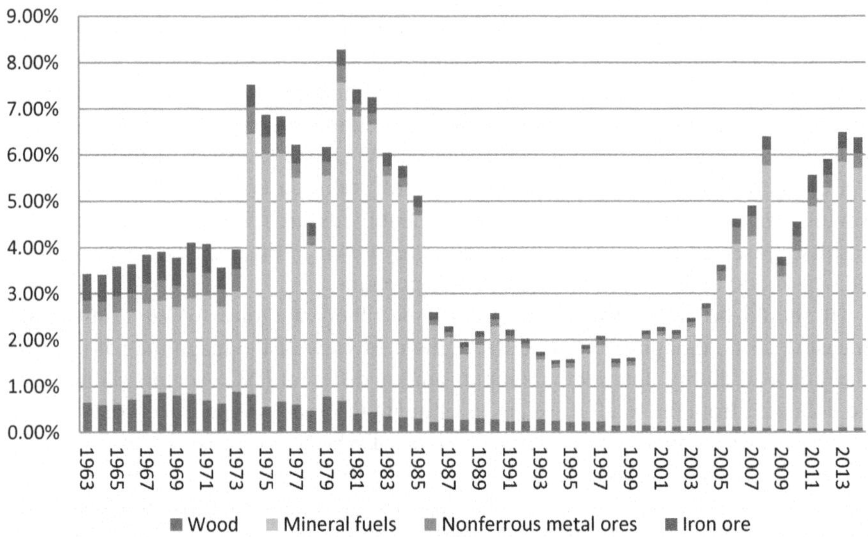

Fig. 7.4 Ratio of rents to output (Estimated as importation value of natural resources)

Third, we consider latent environmental costs. Recognizing the inherent difficulty in evaluating nonmarket values, we conduct a minimum estimation within the extent necessary to observe the general trend in comparison with other environmental costs. Among various possible methodologies, we use the maintenance cost approach highlighted in SEEA 1993, since it is compatible with our definition of

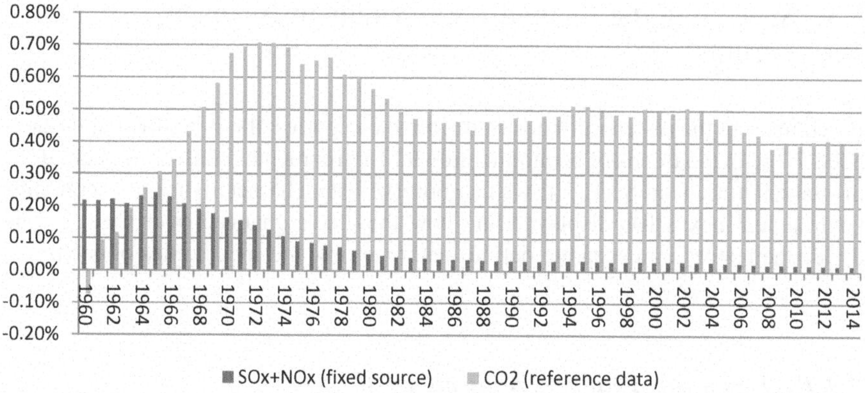

Fig. 7.5 Ratio of latent environmental costs to output (Estimation on selected categories)

this cost as the depletion of natural environment (see Chap. 4).[2] Applying the estimation of imputed environmental costs by Japan Research Institute (1998) as a basis, we conduct a long-term estimation of the cost of sulfur oxides (SO_x) and nitrogen oxides (NO_x) emission (from fixed sources), and that of carbon dioxide (CO_2) emission.[3] The results are presented as shares in the output in Fig. 7.5. The data sources and estimation methods are shown in the appendix.

When interpreting these results, one should note the following. First, while the scope of the estimation is narrowed down for the above-mentioned reasons, the depreciation of natural capital is generated in wider areas, including water and biodiversity issues. These should be taken into consideration when discussing the complete picture of the environmental burdens. Second, the cost of carbon dioxide shown in the figure should be regarded as reference data by which one cannot evaluate the magnitude but instead observe the trend. This is because it is estimated using the unit cost of 6% reduction from 1990 (Kyoto Protocol commitment), under the recognition that an immediate full-scale reduction is impossible and the cost of these CO_2 emissions is immeasurable (Japan Research Institute 1998). Third, the costs of SO_x and NO_x in the figure should also be lower than the real costs caused as damages, because they are estimated as the maintenance costs (i.e., hypothetical costs that would be needed if these types of pollution were to be prevented).

[2]SEEA 1993 proposed the maintenance cost approach, recognizing that it "corresponds to the method of calculating the value of the depreciation of produced fixed assets" (United Nations 1993).

[3]When compared with the estimation by Japanese Research Institute (2004), this estimation extends the timeline so as to cover a long-term and consecutive period, while narrowing the scope to just a few categories of pollutants.

7.3 Specifying the Economy-Environment Nexus by Periods

By comparing the different trends of the three categories of environmental costs in Sect. 7.2 with the trends of economic growth, environmental burdens, and environmental institutions in Sect. 7.1, we can observe what characteristics the economy-environment nexus has displayed and how they have changed over time. Let us divide the history into separate periods and overview the specificities of each.

7.3.1 From the 1960s to Around 1970

From the 1960s to around 1970, the latent environmental costs related to air pollution were continuously high. Those related to CO_2 were initially low, but soared during this period. On the other hand, rents were stable at low levels, and environmental-measure costs remained very low during this period.

These conditions reflect the fact that effective environmental measures were not taken in spite of severe industrial pollution. Moreover, energy prices were also kept low, due to international political and economic conditions, in spite of the increasing consumption of energy and resulting CO_2 emissions.

We can specify the economy-environment nexus in this period as consuming larger amounts of environmental resources (as natural resources and waste-absorption services) that involved latent environmental costs, while both rents and environmental-measure costs were contained due to the institutional factors mentioned above.

7.3.2 From Around 1970 to the Mid-1980s

From around 1970, costs of environmental measures soared, and the latent environmental costs related to air pollution fell. A few years later, rents rose, along with the costs of environmental-measure costs aimed at saving energy, while the latent environmental costs related to CO_2 turned downward.

The former situation reflects the fact that regulatory institutions were introduced through a political process, represented by so-called Pollution Session of the Diet in 1970. It also reflects the energy-saving measures that were strengthened in response to the oil crisis (which was triggered by the policies of oil-producing countries) and the policies introduced to cope with it.

We can specify the economy-environment nexus in this period as two consecutive types of institutional coordination, that is, pollution-abatement regulations followed by energy-saving measures, which raised environmental-measure costs, leading to higher resource efficiency, and thus reduced latent environmental costs and rents.

7.3.3 *From the Mid-1980s to Around 2010*

Starting in the mid-1980s, there was neither a significant increase in environmental-measure costs nor a significant decrease in latent environmental costs related to CO_2. In the 2000s, rents soared due to a rise in resource prices, involving decrease in latent costs, though they fell again around 2010.

These conditions reflect the fact that institutions obligating businesses and other stakeholders to take drastic measures were not formulated, though legislation promoting voluntary actions was actively introduced since the 1990s.

On the other hand, in the 2000s, resource prices soared. This was due to a larger demand in emerging economies, as well as due to an inflow of speculative money. After that, the prices of fossil fuels fell again, indicating that supply constraints of environmental resources appear tighter in the sink than at the source function.

7.4 Concluding Remarks

This chapter, as a first step of the historical analysis, overviewed the long-term trends of the economy-environment nexus in Japan.

First, we looked at the long-term trends of economic growth, environmental burdens, and environmental institutions, which appear to have evolved through their interactions with one another.

Then, to understand more clearly the relationships among them, we conducted a long-term estimation of three kinds of environmental costs: the costs of environmental measures, rents, and latent environmental costs.

By comparing these data and information, we divided the history into three periods— that is, from the 1960s to around 1970, from around 1970 to the mid-1980s, and from the mid-1980s to around 2010—and specified the economy-environment nexus for each period. In short, in the first period, latent environmental costs rose while rents and environmental-measure costs stayed low, showing a delay in the formulation of institutions against pollution. In the second period, environmental-measure costs and rents rose and latent environmental costs decreased, showing strengthened institutions against pollution, as well as the impacts of the oil crisis. In the third period, there were no significant changes in environmental-measure costs and latent environmental costs. This shows that strict institutions such as regulations were not formulated during that time.

Using the estimations and observations in this chapter as a starting point, we proceed with a more detailed analysis in the following chapters. In the next chapter, using the data of environmental-measure costs and rents estimated here, we will conduct an econometric analysis based on the model presented in Chap. 6. The specifications of the economy-environment nexus for each period, briefly discussed above, will be further developed in Chap. 9 to obtain more comprehensive interpretations of the transformation of the economy-environment nexus and growth regimes.

References

Japan Research Institute (1998) Report on estimation of the integrated environmental and economic accounting (in Japanese). Japan Research Institute, Tokyo

Japan Research Institute (2004) Report on reconstruction of the integrated environmental and economic accounting after the revision of SEEA (in Japanese). Japan Research Institute, Tokyo

Okuma K (2016) Long-term transformation of the economy–environment nexus in Japan: a historical analysis of environmental institutions and growth regimes based on the regulation theory. Evol Inst Econ Rev 13:217–237

United Nations (1993) Integrated environmental and economic accounting: interim version. United Nations, New York

Chapter 8
Econometric Analysis of the Impacts of Environmental Measures on Growth

Institutional coordination in the economy-environment nexus, particularly regarding environmental measures, may impact the growth regime. How did the changing economy-environment nexus in Japan, overviewed in the previous chapter, influence the growth regime? Have environmental measures ever positively impacted economic growth? Is there a possibility that such an effect might work even today? In order to answer these questions, this chapter conducts an econometric analysis of Japanese history using a variant of the Kaleckian model developed in Chap. 6, together with the data of environmental costs estimated in Chap. 7.

8.1 Adjusting the Model and Estimating Parameters

In order to conduct an empirical analysis, we first adjust the functions of the model in Chap. 6 (in particular, Sects. 6.2 and 6.3) to fit the econometric analysis of real economies. Assuming that real wage rate is determined by institutional coordination, and thus wage share for production labor ($W_s = wL_p/pY$) is constant in relation to the share of environmental-measure costs (e),[1] we replace θ with zero in the profit function Eq. 6.1.2. Considering the savings from wages, we add $s_w W_s u v_p$ to $s_r r$ in the saving function Eq. 6.2. Accordingly, F_u and F_r are changed into

$$F_u = s_r u v_p - \gamma_u v_p - x_\pi$$

$$F_r = \left(\gamma_u - m_u - s_w W_s v_p\right) u / \pi_p - \left(\gamma_r v_p + x_\pi\right).$$

[1]This assumption is supported by the empirical fact in the 1970s' Japan that the industries' pollution abatement expenses were mostly covered by reduction in other costs and profits (Environment Agency 1992).

K. Okuma, *The Evolving Relationship between Economy and Environment*, Evolutionary Economics and Social Complexity Science 8,
DOI 10.1007/978-981-10-4100-6_8

Then, using the data of environmental-measure costs and rents estimated in Chap. 7, along with economic data such as the profit rate and the rate of capacity utilization (data sources and estimation methods are shown in the appendix), we carried out multiple regressions to estimate parameters. Functions used for estimation and the results of the estimation are shown in Table 8.1.

In this estimation, periods were first set via three major partitions: establishment of the high growth (1963), collapse of the bubble (1991), and the global financial crisis (2008). Second, structural changes were indicated by the results of the CUSUM test and the Stepwise Chow Test for each function.[2] Functions are used without environmental variables when their parameters are not estimated with significance.[3] Results are checked against spurious regression by the unit root test on environmental variables (e, $\Delta E/K$, and T/K) and by a cointegration test on each function.[4]

By calculating the conditions presented in Sects. 6.2 and 6.3 with estimated parameters and other economic data,[5] we can analyze the impacts of environmental-measure costs on capacity utilization rate and profit rate. In particular, we can analyze whether or not the "paradox of cost for environmental measures" worked. Based on the periods set in the estimation above, we analyze two periods: from 1975 to 1982 (1971–1974 and 1983–1987 are also referred to) and from 2001 to 2008.

8.2 Analyzing Regimes in Two Periods: 1975–1982 and 2001–2008

8.2.1 Period Centering on 1975–1982

The period from 1975 to 1982 can be recognized as one that spans the crisis of the growth regime of the high-growth era through the establishment of the export-led regime. The preceding period, from 1971, and the following period, up to 1987, share the same structure as this period in some aspects, such as investment

[2]Results of the Stepwise Chow Test for the rent share function indicate structural changes either in 1982 or in 1985, among which we adopt the former in view of compatibility with other functions.

[3]This model selection is also checked by Akaike information criterion (AIC) or Bayesian information criterion (BIC).

[4]It is noted that there still remains a possibility of the endogeneity problem inherent in simultaneous equation models.

[5]Estimated parameters with a T-ratio of less than 2 are only used as long as their values are plausible and not large enough to disturb the results. For W_s, π, u, and v_p, average values during the periods are used.

Table 8.1 Functions and results of the estimation

a. $S = s_0 + s_r rpK + s_w wL$

Period	s_0	s_r	s_w	ΔR^2	DW
1963–1974	−10,970	0.695	0.365	1.00	1.51
	(−7.40)	(14.16)	(11.82)		
1975–1982	31,794	0.424	0.126	0.97	2.31
	(2.31)	(2.26)	(0.65)		
1983–1991	−45,867	0.654	0.420	1.00	1.91
	(−20.86)	(7.72)	(7.64)		
2001–2008	24,370	0.588	0.026	0.82	1.38
	(0.55)	(3.10)	(0.10)		

b. $g^i = \gamma_0 + \gamma_u u_{-1} + \gamma_r \pi_p v_{p-1} + \gamma_e \Delta E/K$

Period	γ_0	γ_u	γ_r	γ_e	ΔR^2	DW
1971–1987	−0.018	0.037	0.364	11.253	0.99	1.86
	(−0.99)	(1.55)	(13.76)	(6.08)		
1988–1991	−0.159	0.265	0.149	–	0.68	3.15
	(−0.98)	(2.11)	(0.58)			
1992–1997	−0.217	0.287	0.286	–	0.98	2.96
	(−7.67)	(6.63)	(3.39)			
1998–2008	−0.066	0.100	0.337	–	0.81	2.05
	(−3.01)	(3.51)	(3.28)			

c. $m = m_0 + m_{0p}(\text{oilp}) + m_u u - m_e e$

Period	m_0	m_{0p}	m_u	m_e	ΔR^2	DW
1963–1974	0.029	0.043	0.042	–	0.77	1.83
	(1.30)	(6.22)	(1.80)			
1975–1991	0.185	0.016	0.085	18.459	0.97	2.57
	(7.65)	(12.16)	(2.83)	(17.05)		
1996–2008	−0.124	0.015	0.186	–	0.99	1.31
	(−4.57)	(17.26)	(5.84)			

d. $x = x_0 + x_{0w}(\text{worldtr}) + x_{0c}(\text{exchr}) + x_\pi \pi_{p-1} + x_e T/K$

Period	x_0	x_{0w}	x_{0c}	x_π	x_e	ΔR^2	DW
1971–1991	−0.030	0.031	0.020	0.035	0.740	0.94	2.64
	(−1.67)	(3.74)	(5.60)	(1.12)	(5.67)		
1992–2008	−0.010	0.035	−0.002	0.152	–	0.98	2.07
	(−0.74)	(28.85)	(−0.50)	(3.76)			

e. $R_s = R_{s0} + R_{s0p}(\text{oilp}) - \phi e$

Period	R_{S0}	R_{S0p}	φ	ΔR^2	DW
1975–1982	0.210	0.018	16.344	0.88	1.89
	(6.13)	(7.16)	(4.79)		
1982–1991	0.074	0.025	6.225	0.99	2.61
	(2.07)	(15.29)	(2.20)		
1992–2008	0.009	0.019	0.409	1.00	1.46
	(3.02)	(92.42)	(2.07)		

Function of saving (S) instead of that normalized by capital (g_s) is used to obtain significant results

γ_u, γ_r, and x_π are estimated with lags in view of formation of expectation and possible multicollinearity

Some factors are specified by being extracted from constant terms of the original model, that is, *worldtr* world trade normalized by capital, *exchr* exchange rate, *oilp* oil price index

T-ratios are in parentheses; ΔR^2 is adjusted R squared; DW is Durbin–Watson coefficient function.[6] The former can be recognized as one that stretches from the beginning of the crisis to its aggravation by the oil crisis, and the latter as one that runs from the establishment of the growth regime to its development into the bubble economy.

For the whole period from 1971 to 1987, the Keynesian stability condition holds. The intercept of the ED curve is positive.

First, we conduct an analysis within the comparative statics. The value of F_u for the period 1975–1982 is calculated as

$$F_u = s_r u v_p - \gamma_u v_p - x_\pi = -0.028$$

where the sign is negative but the absolute value is small. Further, the value for 1971–1974 is 0.200 and the value for 1983–1987 is 0.116, where the signs are positive.

The value of F_r for the period 1975–1982 is

$$F_r = \left(\gamma_u - m_u - s_w W_s v_p\right) u / \pi_p - \left(\gamma_r v_p + x_\pi\right) = -0.652$$

where the sign is negative. Further, the value for 1971–1974 is (−0.802) and the one for 1983–1987 is (−0.901), where the signs are negative.

Thus, the economy in this period is evaluated as having been in a state where the environmental measures, with the cost-demand effect alone, would pull down the profit rate and probably do the same for capacity utilization. This regime corresponds with exhilarationism, or with conflictive stagnationism that is close to exhilarationism in the Kaleckian taxonomy (Blecker 2002).[7]

Turning to the whole inequalities of conditions including ϕ, m_e, which takes large values after 1975 though it was insignificant before 1974, the left sides of the inequalities 6.12 and 6.15 for the period 1975–1982 show positive large values as

$$F_u(1 - \phi) + m_e = 18.891$$
$$F_r(1 - \phi) + m_e = 28.459.$$

Further, these values for the period 1983–1987 similarly show positive large values.

[6]With variables on environmental costs, investment function is estimated with a high coefficient of determination for the period from 1971 to the mid-1980s, without interruption by the oil crisis in 1974. This result is compatible with the established recognition that the growth regime of the postwar golden era reached its limit not at the oil crisis in 1974 but around 1970, indicating the possibility that the growth regime can be more accurately analyzed by incorporating the environmental aspect.

[7]It should be noted that the regimes identified here are not necessarily the same as those identified by analyses on wage and profit, as environmental costs are not directly saved and their effects are not completely the same as those of wages.

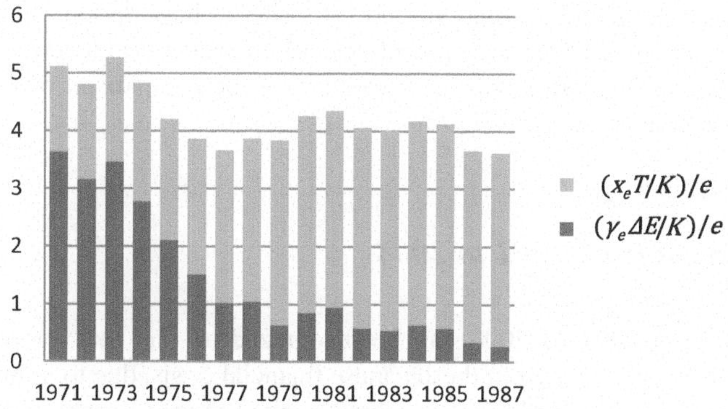

Fig. 8.1 Changing magnitude of dynamic effects

Therefore, for the period from 1975, environmental measures are evaluated as having raised capacity utilization and the profit rate through a large resource-saving effect, showing the paradox of costs for environmental measures.

Next, we analyze the dynamic effects of investment-inducing and export competitiveness. Through the whole period from 1971 to 1987, both γ_e, representing the effect of strengthened environmental measures inducing environmental investment, and x_e, representing the effect of accumulated experiences on environmental measures enhancing export competitiveness, show significant values. These results are compatible with the widely accepted recognition that the environmental measures then resulted in greater investment as well as in higher competitiveness.

When calculating the value of $[(\gamma_e\Delta E/K + x_eT/K)/e]$ (introduced in Sect. 6.3) for each year, it changes stably around four from 1971 to 1987 (Fig. 8.1). The investment-inducing effect appears first and the export competitiveness effect follows, making up the former's decline. Thus, their combined effect works continuously. As long as $[(\gamma_e\Delta E/K + x_eT/K)/e]$ is stable, we can evaluate these dynamic effects by adding its average value to the left side of the inequality of condition 6.15. Using this average for 1975–1982 with assuming $m_e = \phi = 0$ (meaning no resource-saving effect), we obtain

$$F_r + (\gamma_e\Delta E/K + x_eT/K)/e = 3.407$$

showing a positive large value. Further, this value is 4.021 for 1971–1974 and 2.721 for 1983–1987, showing similarly positive large values. Therefore, we can understand that specific categories of environmental measures that do not have resource-saving effects, such as pollution abatements without saving energy, also had positive impacts on the profit rate, exhibiting the paradox of costs for environmental measures.

Finally, again assuming away the dynamic effects discussed above, let us simulate which size of resource-saving effect could have increased the profit rate. Calculating the inequality 6.16 for the period 1975–1982, we obtain $\phi/(1-\phi) > 0.936$, which leads to $\phi > 0.48$. This means that a package of measures with a cost-recovery rate of higher than around 50% should have raised the profit rate, even if we are assuming away the effects of investment-inducing and export competitiveness. This value will be referred to in the comparison of two periods in the next section.

8.2.2 Period from 2001 to 2008

The period from 2001 to 2008 can be recognized as one that spans from the beginning of the recovery from the Japanese financial crisis, due to nonperforming loans, to the global financial crisis triggered by the Lehman Brothers' bankruptcy.

For this period, the Keynesian stability condition holds. The intercept of the ED curve is positive.

The value of F_u is calculated as

$$F_u = s_r u v_p - \gamma_u v_p - x_\pi = -0.057$$

where the sign is negative but the absolute value is small.

The value of F_r is

$$F_r = \left(\gamma_u - m_u - s_w W_s v_p\right) u/\pi_p - \left(\gamma_r v_p + x_\pi\right) = -0.613$$

where the sign is negative.

Thus, the economy in this period is evaluated as in a state in which the environmental measures, with the cost-demand effect alone, will pull down the profit rate and probably do the same for capacity utilization. This corresponds to exhilarationism, which is close to conflictive stagnationism in the Kaleckian taxonomy (Blecker 2002).

Turning to the whole inequalities of conditions including ϕ, m_e, the left sides are

$$F_u(1 - \phi) + m_e = -0.034$$
$$F_r(1 - \phi) + m_e = -0.362.$$

Thus, we can understand that significant resource-saving effects were not observed in this period and the paradox of costs for environmental measures did not work.

Next, looking at the dynamic effects of inducing investment and increasing export, γ_e and x_e are not estimated with statistical significance, which means these effects were not observed. The reason should be that there was no significant increase in environmental-measure costs and thus none in accumulated experiences. If environmental measures had been rapidly strengthened, γ_e and x_e could possibly show significant values, demonstrating the visible effects of inducing investment and increasing export.

Table 8.2 Results of econometric analysis on effects of environmental measures (Okuma 2016)

	Cost-demand effect	Cost-demand effect + Resource-saving effect	Cost-demand effect + Investment-inducing and export-competitiveness effects
	F_r	$F_r(1-\phi)+m_e$	$F_r+(\gamma_e \Delta E/K + x_e T/K)/e$
1971–1974	−0.80	−0.80	4.02
1975–1982	−0.65	28.46	3.41
1983–1987	−0.90	23.17	2.72
Interpretation	Profit rate fell	Profit rate rose by resource-saving effect *Paradox of costs worked*	Profit rate rose by investment-inducing and export competitiveness effects *Paradox of costs worked*
2001–2008	−0.61	−0.36	−0.61
Interpretation	Profit rate fell	Import reduction effect was not statistically significant (Impacts of strengthened measures are unknown.)	Dynamic effects were not statistically significant (Impacts of strengthened measures are unknown.)

Finally, assuming away these dynamic effects, we simulate what kind of environmental measures, in terms of the size of the resource-saving effect, could have increased the profit rate. Calculating the inequality 6.16, we obtain $\phi/(1-\phi) > 1.328$, which leads to $\phi > 0.57$, meaning that a package of measures with a cost-recovery rate of higher than around 60% should have raised the profit rate.[8] When compared to the rate of 50% in the period of 1975–1982, as shown in the previous section, a higher level of cost-recovery rate is required. Though these rates, calculated by this simple model, should not be used as a precise scale to evaluate actual environmental measures, their difference in two periods is clear.

Looking at the parameters in the inequality, this difference is mainly caused by changes in conditions related to trade: that is, import became easier to increase in response to domestic booms (higher m_u), and export became easier to decrease in response to higher costs (higher x_π). Changes in investment conditions also contributed: that is, investment came to be responsive to the profit rate again in the 2000s after having been responsive to capacity utilization in the 1990s (higher γ_r and lower γ_u). Thus, we can understand that the conditions for the paradox of costs for environmental measures became stricter, mainly due to economic globalization and also influenced by its financialization.

An outline of the results of each period discussed above is presented in Table 8.2.

[8] In this period, the parameter of wages in the saving function is estimated to be very small, without statistical significance. This result may be affected by the simultaneous fall of profit and savings in 2008. If this parameter took a larger value, F_r would become smaller, making this condition of cost-recovery rate larger. Even in this case, the main results of this book would not be affected.

8.3 Effects of Future Environmental Measures

Based on the analysis above, we speculate as to whether future environmental measures, if significantly strengthened, can have positive impacts on growth. As the current economic structure is not identified by the analysis above, we assume that it has not significantly changed from the one shown in the period up to 2008.

Environmental-measure costs, similarly to costs in general, can possibly raise capacity utilization and profit rate through the "cost-demand effect." However, this effect alone will probably not raise profit rates under the current economic conditions, as it has become weaker due to the globalization and financialization of the economy.[9] On the other hand, environmental-measure costs, uniquely, have the "resource-saving effect." Since resource saving leads to less importation and to a larger demand in the macroeconomy, environmental measures do not need to recover all of their costs; only some recovery is enough, in order to contribute to a higher profit rate. According to the estimation in Sect. 8.2, the required cost-recovery rate is around 60%.

On the other hand, if environmental measures are strengthened, it is possible that the investment-inducing effect may work in the short term and the export competitiveness effect may work in the mid- to long-term, the combination of which would continuously increase demand. A comparison between the magnitude of these effects in the 1970s (i.e., the value of $[(\gamma_e \Delta E/K + x_e T/K)/e]$) and the parameters representing economic conditions in the 2000s (i.e., the value of F_r), as estimated in Sect. 8.2, indicates that far smaller effects than those in the 1970s, concretely one fifth of them, should contribute to higher profit rates.

The considerations above are on cases either with resource-saving effects, or with effects of inducing investment and increasing export separately. When both of these effects work simultaneously, even smaller magnitudes of combined effects could increase profit rates.

Simulations can be done to understand the magnitude of these effects that is required for the paradox of costs to work. When considering a hypothetical package of environmental measures with a cost-recovery rate of 40% and investment-inducing and export competitiveness effects of 1/20 of those observed in the 1970s, the inequality of conditions incorporating the dynamic effects is calculated as

$$F_r(1-\phi) + m_e + (\gamma_e \Delta E/K + x_e T/K)/e = 0.02 > 0$$

which would positively impact the profit rate.

[9]The most important element of the cost-demand effect is higher total wages caused by more employment in environmental sectors (the ESGS sector). Advocates of the "Green New Deal" or "Green Growth" often emphasize the effects of job creation. The result of our analysis indicates that higher employment in the environmental sectors alone will probably not enable higher growth. However, higher employment should still have significant importance when taking into consideration the aspects of social stability, as well as the long-term productivity improved by working experiences.

Here, let us speculate to what extent these effects are able to work in today's circumstances. Regarding the resource-saving effect, we can expect a potentially large effect when taking into consideration the fact that many of greenhouse gas reduction measures are said to be economically viable in the longer term (Central Environmental Policy Council 2010), though this expectation may be affected by unclear future trends in fossil fuel prices, under expected global economic growth on the one hand and the recent development of shale oils on the other.

Regarding the investment-inducing effect, a considerable effect can be expected in view of current economic conditions in Japan, where demand-supply gaps exist and financial assets are not adequately utilized for investments. Its scale may, however, be smaller than that in the 1970s because a certain portion of investment demand will be filled by importation (i.e., leakage of the effect), one example of which includes the importation of solar panels. Regarding the export competitiveness effect, a considerable effect can again be expected, taking into consideration that many environmental measures depend on machine and other industries where Japan holds an advantage, though its scale may also be smaller than before since there are areas where other countries have already established superior positions. One example of this is the windmill industry.

Based on these considerations, we can safely say that, although the cost-demand effect became weaker under the globalized economy, if environmental measures are strengthened with attention to the effects of saving resources, inducing environmental investments, and enhancing export competitiveness, these effects combined will likely bring about the paradox of costs for environmental measures, which indicates the probability of Green Growth.

8.4 Concluding Remarks

This chapter has conducted an econometric analysis, using a Kaleckian model presented in Chap. 6, in order to understand how environmental measures in Japan have impacted its economic growth.

We conducted the analysis on two periods: one centering on 1975–1982 and another from 2001 to 2008, which were set by structural changes indicated by the econometric test.

In the period from 1975 to 1982, it was shown that environmental measures raised the profit rate through significant effects of reducing importation of resources, inducing environmental investments, and enhancing export competitiveness. This shows that the paradox of costs for environmental measures worked.

In the period from 2001 to 2008, environmental measures were not so strengthened as to increase their costs, and thus their effect of increasing profit rate was not observed. Under the globalization of the economy, conditions for the paradox of costs became stricter than in the 1970s.

However, it was indicated that if environmental measures were strengthened and the effects of resource saving, inducing investment, and export competitiveness worked, their combined effect would likely lead to higher profit rate, realizing Green Growth.

The analysis of this chapter is based on the economic structure of Japan until around 2010, due to data constraints. After that, the Japanese economy was impacted by the Great East Japan Earthquake and then by Abenomics, and its structure may have been changed. The terms of this analysis are left to be extended as related data become available.

References

Blecker RA (2002) Distribution, demand and growth in neo-Kaleckian macro models. In: Setterfield M (ed) The economics of demand-led growth: challenging the supply-side vision of the long run. Edward Elgar, Northampton, pp 129–152

Central Environment Policy Council (2010) Interim report on vision of policies and measures to achieve the mid- to long-term emission reduction targets (in Japanese). http://www.env.go.jp/council/06earth/y0611-19.html. Accessed 25 Nov 2016

Environment Agency (1992) Quality of the environment in Japan, 1992. Environment Agency, Tokyo

Okuma K (2016) Long-term transformation of the economy–environment nexus in Japan: a historical analysis of environmental institutions and growth regimes based on the regulation theory. Evol Inst Econ Rev 13:217–237

Chapter 9
Interpreting the Historical Transformation

So far, we have overviewed the trend of economy-environment relationship by referring to indices (Chap. 7) and have analyzed the impacts of environmental measures on the economy by using a model (Chap. 8). By applying these results, together with further information on environmental institutions and their formation processes, we can interpret the historical transformation of the relationship between economy and the environment in Japan.

We will now periodize the history from the 1960s to today, and analyze the specificities of the relationship in each period. For each period, we will identify the nature of the economy-environment nexus, paying attention to the dynamics of institutional coordination and the size of the environmental costs, and consider its interaction with growth regimes. Through a series of such periodized specifications, we will be able to understand the historical transformation.

Japanese postwar history is divided into five periods: (1) from the 1960s to around 1970; (2) from around 1970 to the early 1980s; (3) from the early 1980s to around 1990; (4) from the 1990s to around 2008; and (5) after around 2008. Let us go through the history by analyzing each period.

9.1 The 1960s to Around 1970

9.1.1 Institutional Coordination in the Economy-Environment Nexus

In the postwar era of worldwide economic growth (called the golden era of capitalism), Japan's growth rate was particularly high among the developed countries. This rapid growth was supported by mass production and mass consumption,

K. Okuma, *The Evolving Relationship between Economy and Environment*,
Evolutionary Economics and Social Complexity Science 8,
DOI 10.1007/978-981-10-4100-6_9

which involved expanding the consumption of natural resources and energy as well as the emission of pollutants.

This caused industrial pollution in many regions. For example, in Minamata city, a prominent chemical cooperation caused water pollution by organic mercury, inciting severe health damages. In Yokkaichi city, a petrochemical complex, built as a national project, caused severe air pollution. Big businesses, as well as national policies for industrial development, caused severe local pollution.

In polluted areas, residents suffering from the pollution stood up, advocating for the prohibition of such emissions, though neither businesses nor the government readily took effective action. Industries, the ministry responsible for industrial policy, and even some scientists opposed countermeasures, arguing that the causations were not clear (Kawana 1987). Miyamoto (1989) emphasized that "exogenous developments" neglecting local residents' benefits lead to pollution problems. Local actors requesting countermeasures were barely able to make their voices heard at the national policy level. Faced with the power and influence of actors that were against the countermeasures, institutional coordination did not proceed.

There were spatial gaps between local communities and big businesses, as well as with the central government, that caused this delay of countermeasures. This exemplifies the "spatial and temporal gap of coordination" presented in Sect. 5.1.

However, there were still some cases where countermeasures were taken under coordination between victims and polluters. For example, the "Honshu paper incident" occurred in 1958. Fishermen working in Tokyo's Edo River, who suffered from the effects of wastewater from a paper factory, resorted to intruding into the factory. This stimulated the government to quickly enact legislations for water quality management (called the "two water-quality laws"), although these proved not to be effective enough (Kawana 1987). There was little spatial gap between related actors, with both groups being located in the capital city of Tokyo, which appears to have contributed to the relatively quick coordination. In Ube city in Yamaguchi prefecture, a heavy industry corporation locally developed from coal mining caused air pollution. This pollution was overcome at a relatively early stage by local regulations that were voluntarily agreed upon among stakeholders (called the "Ube method") (Kawana 1987). The reason for this success probably lies in the very small spatial gaps among the locally developed corporation, city government, and citizens, which enabled local coordination.

On the other hand, the increasing consumption of energy was expanding CO_2 emissions beyond the ecosystem's ability to absorb them, though the consequences of this were not yet scientifically clear. It was also reducing reserves of exhaustible resources such as oil, though that was compensated by the development of new oil wells in the Middle East, and oil prices were kept low under the international economic regime.

Consequently, as seen in Chap. 7, environmental-measure costs did not increase significantly. In addition, rent represented by the import value of oil did not increase either. On the other hand, the latent environmental costs related to pollutants such as sulfur oxides were continuously high, and the ones related to greenhouse gasses were also rapidly increasing.

As described above, the economy-environment nexus in this period was characterized by low rent and environmental-measure costs, vis-a-vis the high latent environmental costs. The reason for this was the delayed formulation of institutions, in spite of increasing resource consumption and pollutant emissions. We call this form of the economy-environment nexus "environmental-resources mass-consumption with low cost type."

9.1.2 Interaction with the Growth Regime

Now, we consider the interaction between this economy-environment nexus and the growth regime. In this period, the Fordist growth regime was functioning in developed countries, and was characterized by a cumulative causation of increasing production and improving productivity (see Sect. 5.3). In Japan, a high level of investment supported by high profit rates was driving this mechanism.[1]

This cumulative causation required mass-production, which involved both mass-consumption of natural resources and mass-emission of wastes. However, rent and environmental-measure costs were suppressed, which ensured profit leading to high levels of investment. Thus, the economy-environment nexus of this type contributed to the growth regime in this period.

The concept of Fordism was built without incorporating the environmental aspect, thus far. However, when putting away the traditional assumption of abundant nature and taking into consideration the economy-environment nexus as the sixth institutional form, the Fordist growth regime can be recognized as being partly supported by the economy-environment nexus of environmental-resources mass-consumption with low cost type.

As described above, the economy-environment nexus of this type was compatible with the growth regime in this period, constituting one element of the mode of *régulation*. However, mass-consumption of resources and mass-emission of wastes cannot be continued forever, since there are limits to the capacity of nature both in resource-supply and waste-absorption functions. Eventually, rents as compensation to damages or resource prices, and/or costs of environmental measures to mitigate them, must rise, reducing profit. Thus, this growth regime has endogenous mechanisms leading to crisis. These limits had not yet become apparent to the production system due to the spatial gap of coordination, though they were to become evident in the form of required environmental measures and the oil crisis in the next period.

[1]It should be noted that there are various views on the Fordist regime in Japan as to whether it was working, and if so, what type it was (Yamada 2008).

9.2 The 1970s to the Early 1980s

9.2.1 Institutional Coordination in the Economy-Environment Nexus

In the late 1960s, faced with severe pollution, local anti-pollution campaigns proliferated and legal cases were presented. For example, in Yokkaichi city, local residents suffering health damages, such as asthma, launched a protest campaign in the early 1960s and brought a lawsuit to court in 1967. In Mishima city, Numazu city, and Shimizu town in Shizuoka prefecture, local residents undertook a campaign against the planned petrochemical complex and conducted effective activities, including a counterargument based on their own scientific research against the scientific committee sent in by the Ministry of International Trade and Industry (MITI). This led to the abolishment of the plan in 1964 (Kawana 1987; Miyamoto 1989).

These local residents' campaigns gradually acquired support from scientists, mass media, and wider public opinions, and finally came to be a priority issue within national politics. In 1970, the Diet session devoted to discussions on anti-pollution policies (the so-called "Pollution Session of the Diet") was held, and 14 legislations for this purpose, either new or amended, were adopted. Among them were amendments of the Basic Law for Pollution Control and the Air Pollution Prevention Law, and the establishment of the Water Pollution Prevention Law and the Waste Management Law, by which regulations were significantly tightened (see Table 7.1 in Chap. 7). Moreover, the Environment Agency was established, based on the decision of the then Prime Minister Sato in 1971 (Environment Agency 1991). This means that, in the coordination mechanism among actors, an actor representing the benefit of the environment and victims of pollution was generated within the government. Since then, the Environment Agency, pushed by claims from victims, has negotiated with industry and strengthened the regulations. Examples include the introduction of "total emission control" and the strict standards on automobile exhaust (the so-called "Japanese Muskie Act") (Kawana 1988).

Miyamoto (1989) summarized the progress in this period, in Japanese, as "local residents' opinions and campaigns, with support from the mass media and international public opinions and through anti-pollution lawsuits and local government reforms, changed the policy of the government." We understand that democratic mechanisms, such as the judicial system and mass media, filled the spatial gap of coordination between the environmental interests represented by local communities and national politics, enabling the formulation of institutions.

On the other hand, triggered by the Middle East War, oil-exporting countries tightened control over its production, causing the first and second oil crises. Oil prices soared and so did the production costs of industries.

In response, businesses made efforts to reduce energy consumption, which the government supported through tax exemptions, loans, and subsidies using new legislation. These energy-saving measures not only reduced consumption of fossil fuels and greenhouse gas emissions, but also contributed to reducing emissions of other pollutants (Environment Agency 1981).

Consequently, as we saw in Chap. 7, the costs of environmental measures significantly rose around 1970–1980, and rent as oil import value also soared in the late 1970s. Accordingly, latent environmental costs of pollutants such as SO_x fell and those of CO_2 turned downward.

As described above, in the economy-environment nexus in this period, institutional coordination, driven originally by antipollution campaigns, raised costs of environmental measures. Later, international political coordination raised the rent of energy resources as well as the environmental-measures costs for energy-saving, both of which reduced latent environmental costs. We recognize this economy-environment nexus as a mixture of pollution abatement and energy-saving, and call it "pollution regulation and energy-saving type."

9.2.2 Interaction with the Growth Regime

Next, we look at the interaction of this form of economy-environment nexus with the growth regime. The so-called Fordist growth regime reached its limit around 1970, due to the saturated domestic market of durable consumer goods and increased wages. Thus, the economy went into a crisis until a new growth regime was formed in the early 1980s, characterized by export and the investment it induced (Uemura 2000). How did the economy-environment nexus impact these changing regimes?

The econometric analysis in Chap. 8 shows that increasing environmental-measure costs in this period had a positive impact on economic growth through the resource-saving effect, that is, the effect of reducing the import of energy resources by reducing energy consumption. It also indicates that even pollution-abatement measures without resource-saving effects positively impacted economic growth, through their effects of inducing environmental investment and enhancing export competitiveness. These results mean that the "paradox of costs for environmental measures" worked in this period (see Sect. 5.3). There has already been widely accepted recognition that strict environmental regulations in this period had positive impacts, rather than negative ones, on the economy by inducing investments in pollution-control plants and equipment, as well as through enhancing competitiveness by stimulating technological improvements. One example of this is the automobile incineration technologies stimulated by strict emission standards (OECD 1991; Environment Agency 1992). The results of the analysis above are consistent with this discourse.

Thus, we can understand that the economy-environment nexus in this period had an effect of smoothing the transition from the crisis of the growth regime of the

1960s to the formation of the next growth regime of the 1980s. This was achieved by reducing the import of energy resources, underpinning the bottom of the recession by pollution-abatement investments in the short-term, and contributing to technological competitiveness in the midterm. This can be recognized as an example of Green Growth, as shown by the experience of pollution control in Japan.

As we saw in the previous section, the Fordist growth regime of the postwar era had an endogenous mechanism of raising environmental costs through its attributes of mass production and consumption. Even behind the apparently external oil crisis was an endogenous factor of expanding consumption of energy. Thus, the economy-environment nexus of "environmental-resources mass-consumption with low cost type" reached its limit and changed into the next form of "pollution control and energy-saving type." Under this new economy-environment nexus, emissions of traditional pollutants were significantly reduced and energy consumption was also controlled. However, as shown in the continued latent environmental costs, CO_2 emission beyond the absorption abilities of the ecosystem was still continuing. This means that the growth in this period continued to have an extensive nature in terms of consumption of environmental resources, involving the endogenous mechanism leading to crisis in the future.

9.3 The Late 1980s

9.3.1 Institutional Coordination in the Economy-Environment Nexus

While severe industrial pollution became alleviated, continued mass-production and mass-consumption caused the so-called "urban and lifestyle-related pollution," for example, air pollution by automobile exhaust. In such types of pollution, polluters and victims are sparsely spread in wider economic activities, and the pressure from anti-pollution campaigns became weaker compared to those against industrial pollution.

Environmental policy lost its driving forces in political coordination, and institutional development became stagnated. One symbolic case was the bill of environmental impact assessment, which was proposed to the Diet several times but was finally discarded in 1983 due to opposition from industries, MITI and allied politicians (Environment Agency 1991; Kawana 1995).

Under such circumstances, costs of environmental measures (in terms of ratio to output) stopped increasing. We understand this period as a stagnation of institutional development.

9.4 The 1990s to the Early 2000s

9.4.1 Institutional Coordination in the Economy-Environment Nexus

As a result of continued mass-production and mass-consumption, waste disposal problems and global environmental problems became evident in the late 1980s. Expanding solid wastes gave rise to a severe shortage of landfill sites in Japan. Concerns mounted about global problems such as climate change and declining tropical forests, and international movements became active, of which the Earth Summit in 1992 was the typical example.

Under such circumstances, citizens' organizations and scientists emerged as new kinds of actors supporting environmental interests. For example, in addition to traditional citizens' organizations around nature conservation, those promoting eco-friendly activities such as recycling emerged. More scientists started to sound the alarm on the global environmental crisis. On the waste disposal issue, local governments responsible for waste disposal administration also became influential actors requesting reduction of wastes to businesses.

Moreover, there also emerged influential politicians interested in global environmental issues, partly stimulated by the international circumstances where these issues were on the agenda of summit meetings. For example, one-time Prime Minister Takeshita played an influential role in promoting environmental policies: he worked as the president of an important international conference discussing financial issues in the lead-up to the Earth Summit, and led a committee in the ruling party discussing the establishment of the basic legislation of the environmental policy (Kawana 1995).[2]

Emergence of these new actors led to the formulation of institutions to promote environmental measures. For example, the Basic Environment Law was enacted in 1993. Its momentum was led by the above-mentioned committee in the ruling party and eventually by its direction to the relevant ministries by the then Prime Minister Miyazawa (Environment Agency 1994). This basic law also paved the way to the enactment of the Environmental Impact Assessment Law in 1997.

In the field of waste management policy, against the background of requests from local governments and increasing awareness of citizens, several legislations to promote reduction and recycling of wastes were formulated. Starting from the amendment of the Waste Disposal Law and the enactment of the Recycled Resources Utilization Law, both in 1990, legislation for the recycling of specific products was consecutively developed: the Container and Packaging Recycling Law in 1995, the Electric Appliances Recycling Law in 1998, and the Automobile Recycling Law in 2002. The framework legislation of these laws, that is,, the Basic

[2]Behind this political leadership were said to be not only a personal awareness of high levels of environmental problems, but also an intention to extend their political powers into emerging policy areas and potential businesses (Murai 2001).

Law for Establishing the Recycling-Based Society, was enacted in 2000 (see Table 7.1 in Chap. 7). As a result of negotiations among stakeholders, these laws were enacted as systems of promoting voluntary actions of producers by showing guidelines or obligating recycling with the costs borne largely by consumers. These are characteristic of Japan legislation, compared to those of European countries that emphasize producers' responsibilities (Okuma 2006).

Institutions to address global warming were also developed. In response to the adoption of the Kyoto Protocol, The Global Warming Mitigation Law was enacted and the Energy-Saving Law was strengthened simultaneously in 1998. Since then, these two laws have been simultaneously amended, keeping pace with international institutional progress: that is, they were amended in 2002 when the protocol was ratified, in 2005 when it entered into force, and in 2008 when its First Commitment Period started (see Table 7.1 in Chap. 7). The "Voluntary Action Plan" was also established by the Federation of Economic Organizations in 1997, to which the governmental plan for greenhouse gas reduction effectively delegated the decision of reduction targets and measures of industrial sectors.

The Global Warming Mitigation Law originally stipulated a planning scheme of national and local governments, promotion of actions of citizens, etc., and has been strengthened step by step. On the other hand, regulations, carbon tax, and tradable permits were not introduced in this period, owing to opposition from businesses and METI (Ministry of Economy, Trade and Industry), who argued that business actions should be promoted voluntarily by the above-mentioned action plan (Central Environment Policy Council 2001). The Energy-Saving Law stipulated schemes of promoting business actions through showing guidelines of factory operations and products, and also has been strengthened by widening the target businesses and introducing performance criteria on automobiles and appliances.

In addition, against the background of increasing awareness of consumers and some leading companies, schemes of corporate environmental management and green procurement also became widespread.

These institutions, when compared with regulations in the 1970s, emphasized cooperation and shared roles among a wide range of actors, including consumers, as well as a voluntary and flexible nature in terms of business activities. One of the reasons for such characteristics is said to have been the need to address a wider range of economic activities causing environmental loads. Another reason was the greater importance of support and consent from businesses, in a context where the pressures from actors on behalf of the environment were weaker compared with the antipollution campaigns of the 1970s. In the case of global environmental problems, gaps between polluters and victims (e.g., the gap between industrialized/industrializing countries and island states, or the one between current generations and future generations) weaken the pressure from actors and thus the strength of institutions.

Consequently, the costs of environmental measures did not significantly increase in this period. Latent environmental costs were also almost stable, as CO_2 continued to be emitted far beyond nature's absorption capacities (see Chap. 7).

As described above, in the economy-environment nexus in this period, institutions emphasizing voluntariness and flexibility, while not involving a significant increase in environmental-measure costs, were formulated under the coordination based on the awareness of a wide range of stakeholders. We call this economy-environment nexus simply the "voluntary measure type."

9.4.2 Interaction with Mode of **Régulation** *and the Growth Regime*

Now, we will look at the relationship of this economy-environment nexus with the mode of *régulation* and the growth regime. In the institutional form of the wage-labor nexus, the employment system became more flexible (e.g., increasing nonregular workers) under the fierce international competition after the mid-1990s (Uemura 2011). This is understood as constraints imposed by the dominant institutional form in the "institutional hierarchy". The emphasis on voluntariness and flexibility to businesses in the economy-environment nexus was in line with this change in the wage-labor nexus. Thus, we consider that "institutional complementarities" under the "institutional hierarchy" dominated by international competition partly explain the above characteristics of the economy-environment nexus (see Sect. 5.2).

In the early 2000s, Japan experienced a growth pattern led by exports (Uemura 2011). Under this type of economy-environment nexus, costs of environmental measures did not significantly increase, which appears to have been compatible with the growth pattern by contributing to curbing production costs. However, when looking at some environment-related products, such as solar panels, windmills, and biomass boilers, Japanese manufacturing lagged behind that of countries with stricter institutions, which may have negative implications on future growth.

9.5 After 2008

9.5.1 Institutional Coordination in the Economy-Environment Nexus

Faced with the global economic crisis triggered by the subprime problems, and backed by the international momentum for climate change policy gained in the UN negotiation process toward a new agreement, which it planned to reach by 2009, ideas of Green Growth or a Green New Deal were advocated by high-level politicians in many states, including Japan. This can be understood as an initiative formulated under cooperation between actors supporting economic interests and those supporting environmental ones.

In Japan, large-scale subsidies were introduced for ecologically friendly automobiles and energy-efficient electric appliances as a temporary financial stimulus. On the other hand, institutions that involved an increase in production costs were not readily introduced, in the face of opposition. Still, they gradually started to be introduced, influenced by the progress in other countries and partly by political circumstances, including the change of governing party. The feed-in tariff system was established in July 2012, and the carbon tax system in October 2012. Since then, renewable energies and energy-saving measures have been promoted by the feed-in tariff system as well as by policies utilizing carbon tax revenues (see Table 7.1 in Chap. 7).

As described above, in the economy-environment nexus in this period, environmental measures, as a simultaneous in pursuit of economic and environmental benefit, have been explored based on cooperation between economic and environmental actors. We call this currently developing economy-environment nexus the "green-growth-oriented type," as a tentative specification.

On the other hand, the Great East Japan earthquake and the nuclear accident in 2011 gave a severe shock to the Japanese economy and society, and impacted environmental policy as well. Suspension of most nuclear power plants has encouraged energy-savings throughout the economy, while forcing reconsideration of the greenhouse gas reduction policy. Severe experiences of the natural disaster are said to have changed people's minds in favor of an autonomous and distributed system of energy supply and other economic activities.

Policies of the Abe administration have been placing great emphasis on economic growth, an example of which is the catchphrase of "Abenomics." Unprecedented policies of monetary easing are under way and the structure of the economy may possibly be changing.

On the other hand, as a new global framework to mitigate climate change, the Paris Agreement was adopted in COP 21 of the United Nations' Framework Convention of Climate Change, held in December 2015. This stipulates worldwide targets of 2 °C and obligates contracting countries to submit their targets and measures, though not regulating the emissions of each country. In response, the Japanese government decided on the Plan for Global Warming Countermeasures in May 2016, stipulating the target of reducing 26% of GHGs in 2030 (compared to 2013), which indicates that environmental measures need to be significantly strengthened from now on.

It is not clear at this stage how these recent developments will change the economy-environment nexus, and whether the "green-growth-oriented type" will stand and continue.

9.5.2 Interaction with the Growth Regime

Although it is too early to evaluate the impact of this preliminary economy-environment nexus on the growth regime, we will try to make tentative considerations to the extent possible at this stage.

The subsidies mentioned above raised the sales of automobiles and electric appliances, which worked as stimulus measures under the recession (Ministry of the Environment et al. 2011). However, these measures cannot last long under budgetary constraints.

On the other hand, environmental measures involving increasing production costs (e.g. regulations, taxes and charges), if implemented, could form a lasting institution. As mentioned above, such measures in the 1970s gave a positive impetus to growth through the paradox of costs. Although the conditions of this paradox became stricter in the 2000s, there will be a good probability for environmental measures to impact positively on growth if implemented in such a way that their effects of resource-saving, investment-inducing, and export competitiveness are enhanced (see Sect. 8.3).

Institutional coordination with the above-mentioned measures, if any, needs to be formulated as a compromise among actors. Here we review the present states of actors in Japan to see the possibility of such coordination.

Regarding global environmental problems, we have not seen such strong pressures from citizens or other actors as to formulate strict institutions, since people who suffer from their impact are located in spatially or temporally remote places (i.e., the spatial or temporal gap of coordination). There are companies gradually recognizing environmental degradations and criticisms from NGOs as risks for their businesses, though business associations are arguing for deregulation in labor policies as well as a supply of cheaper energy, both in order to reduce costs. In view of these conditions, it is not probable that such institutional coordination could be realized with the actors on the environment side overwhelming the business voices. A more probable scenario would be that it is achieved under cooperation among relevant actors without confronting profit and growth.

Here, it should be noted that this coordination is beyond the scope of past cooperation among economic and environmental actors. The economy-environment nexus of "voluntary measure type" in the 1990s did not involve a significant rise in environmental-measure costs. However, the positive impact on the economy will be paradoxically generated by the apparent negative impact of rising costs on businesses (i.e. "paradox of costs"). The feasibility of such institutional coordination will depend on how wide the scope of the cooperation extends, as well as on how powerful new environmental actors become.

9.5.3 Emerging Trends Searching for New Coordination

In this period, we see some movements emerging that seek institutional coordination by new mechanisms of governance, other than traditional state governments or international agreements. Let us overview a couple of such new trends.

First, some emerging movements are trying to directly influence the globalizing economy. These originate from USA- or Europe-based organizations and are gaining international influence. Some international environmental NGOs have started to run campaigns targeted to large multinational companies. They investigate environmental and social problems, including those within the supply chains of these companies. They then urge them to improve their operations, call for consumers to boycott their products, and also commend good practices when improved.[3] Behind these actions is a tactic to influence the wider economy, including small or foreign companies, through the supply chains of big businesses. NGOs have also started to request companies to disclose environmental information such as CO_2 emissions, so that this information is taken into consideration by investors and thus changes the money flow. These can be regarded as activities that aim to directly impact the global economy by connecting the awareness of citizens to big businesses.

Companies and investors are also gradually recognizing environmental issues as important risk factors as well as opportunities for their businesses. Some institutional investors, such as pension funds, have started to make investment decisions referring not only to financial performance but also to performance in the environmental, social, and governance aspects (called "ESG investment"). Some have also started to consider withdrawing investments from businesses relying on fossil fuels, in recognition of "carbon risks" under probable CO_2 reductions. Having started with US and European investors, these actions are coming to be seen worldwide, including in Japan. For example, the Government Pension Investment Fund of Japan (GPIF; the world's largest institutional investor) decided to start ESG investments in 2016.

The second trend is toward activities to create sustainable communities in local regions. There are emerging efforts to revitalize local regions by developing products that utilize natural capital, such as renewable energy, organic agricultures sustainable fisheries, and so on. Projects are often financed by citizens, local companies, and local banks, so that profits are reinvested locally, creating local economic circulation. In Japan, local projects around renewable energies have emerged from around 2000, and have been activated since the introduction of the feed-in tariff system in 2012. Examples include a series of citizen-funded wind power projects led by an organization in Hokkaido, a system of promoting locally led projects under the collaboration of local government and citizens' organizations in Iida city (Nagano prefecture), and newly emerging companies led by citizens and local businesses developing locally beneficial projects in Fukushima prefecture, Tokushima prefecture, etc. Cooperation and information-sharing among projects are also active, leading to the establishment of large-scale networking organizations.[4] The government has also been promoting renewable energy projects, with an

[3]For example, Greenpeace ran a campaign in 2010 calling for a boycott on Nestlé products, saying that the palm oil used therein was causing deforestation in Indonesia. This made Nestlé establish a procurement policy to use sustainable resources. They also urged other global companies using palm oil to take appropriate actions and evaluated them in a ranking.

[4]An example of such organizations is the Japan Community Power Association, established in 2014.

emphasis on locally led ones.[5] Some recognize these projects as movements to generating a new domain of the economy locally, apart from the global one.[6]

These movements from the global to the local scale aim to influence the economy through routes other than the traditional governance system of states or international organizations. These efforts are noteworthy, in terms of seeking ways to strengthen environmental institutions under the globalizing economy. However, most of them utilize institutions of state governments or international agreements as their basis (e.g., expectations of strict regulations in the future to evaluate business risks, feed-in tariff systems to enable locally led projects, etc.), and only a few can run independently. It is not yet clear how great the effects of these movements can be, in a context where it is difficult to strengthen traditional institutions.

9.6 Long-Term Transformation

The periodized specifications of the economy-environment nexus, described in Sects. 9.1, 9.2, 9.3, 9.4, and 9.5 above, can be summarized as in Table 9.1. The economy-environment nexus was formulated through coordination between the actors characteristic of each period, resulting in its specific types being reflected in environmental costs. This impacted the growth regime of the period, showing some forms of compatibility.

The economy-environment nexus has changed over time, interacting with crises of growth regime and influenced by the changing institutional hierarchy in the mode of *régulation*. This is a process of historical evolution, forming part of the longer-term world history described in Chap. 2. In concluding this chapter, let us overview the longer-term evolution, extending the scope to the history of capitalism.

In the nineteenth century, an extensive growth regime functioned by subsuming a large quantity of labor forces with low wages, as well as by obtaining new places for resource acquisition and marketing by means of colonies or frontiers. However, at the beginning of the twentieth century, faced with a curbed labor supply and inadequate demand, the world economy went into a period of crisis (Boyer 1986).[7]

In the latter half of the twentieth century (after the Second World War), a new institutional coordination in the wage-labor nexus was formulated. This enabled higher productivity and higher wages, supporting a stable growth regime and realizing the "golden era of capitalism" (ibid.). This was called an intensive growth

---

[5]For example, the Japanese Ministry of the Environment has been promoting locally led renewable energy projects by various policies, including the establishment of a fund (the Green Fund) to invest in such projects.

[6]Motani et al. (2013) introduced various locally led projects generating values by utilizing natural resources in countryside forest areas ("Satoyama" in Japanese), calling them "Satoyama capitalism."

[7]More precisely, there was a short period of an unstable regime of "intensive accumulation without mass-consumption" after the First World War (Boyer 1986).

Table 9.1 Periodized specifications of the economy-environment nexus in Japan

Periods	1960s	1970s to early 1980s	Late 1980s	1990s to early 2000s	After 2008
Types of Economy-environment nexus	**Environmental-resources mass-consumption with low cost type**	**Pollution regulation and energy-saving type**	**(Stagnation of institution)**	**Voluntary measure type**	**Green-growth-oriented type?**
Dynamics of institutional coordination	Insufficient measures due to gaps of coordination.	Local campaigns led to state political issues, and pollution regulation introduced.	Weaker actors for environment	Wider environmental concerns led to voluntary measures.	Cooperation between actors led to stimulus measures.
Status of environmental costs	Low EMC and rent; higher latent cost.	EMC and rent rise; Latent cost reduced.	EMC stop rising.	No significant change in EMC and latent cost.	Measures that increase EMC also gradually introduced.
Effects on growth regime	Contributed to high profit by containing environmental costs under mass production.	Contributed to transition to the next regime via resource-saving, investment, and competitiveness effects.		Compatible with competitive international regime by containing costs. Less effect of technical competitiveness.	Future effects depend on resource-saving, investment, and competitiveness effects.
Growth regime	**Fordism**		**Export- led**	**(Export-led in 2000s)**	

EMC is environmental-measure cost

regime, which did not involve an extensive increase in labor input. However, it did require mass-production and mass-consumption, involving an extensive increase in the input of environmental resources. Thus, it has an inherent mechanism that leads it into crisis when it reaches its limit in the environmental aspect.

Because of the nature of environmental degradations, whose damages tend to occur in remote places or in the future, these limits did not became evident at once but gradually emerged with some time lags.

In the 1970s, a part of this limit became visible through local campaigns against pollution and the oil crisis, leading to the formulation of institutions for pollution abatement and energy-saving. However, mass-production and mass-consumption continued, involving large-scale waste generation and CO_2 emission.

The limit gradually became evident in the form of global environmental problems. In the 1990s, public awareness on environmental issues, as well as international momentum, pushed for the formulation of environmental institutions. However, at that time, competitive institutional forms became prevalent under the globalizing economy. This forced the deregulation of labor institutions and also required voluntariness and flexibility to become a part of environmental institutions' agreements. Such institutions managed to somewhat restrain the increasing trend of energy and resource consumption, although the amount of consumption continues to be beyond the reproductive capacity of the natural environment, meaning continued extensive growth in terms of consumption of the natural capital.

As described above, we have never seen a growth regime not involving extensive growth in both the aspects of labor and environmental resource usage. However, the economy of human beings has already exceeded the limits, in terms of consumption of environmental resources, and it must be forced to change into an economy without extensive growth, someday and somehow. If institutional coordination is further delayed and degradation continues to be exacerbated, then costs for the compensation of damages or adaptation to the degraded environment will expand, meaning an even harder eventual landing.

On the other hand, it should be noteworthy that the strict pollution abatement and energy-savings in the 1970s positively impacted economic growth in Japan by reducing the import of energy resources, inducing investment in the short-term, and contributing to exports through technological improvements in the mid- to long term. This can be seen as an example of Green Growth. It was also shown that, even today, there is a good chance that strict environmental measures could again contribute to growth. However, such an institutional coordination will require new social compromises and commitment. Moreover, it is still questionable if such coordination could bring us all the way to a sustainable economy, without extensive consumption of the environment.

9.7 Concluding Remarks

This chapter, by synthesizing the results of previous chapters, has interpreted the long-term transformation of the relationship between economy and the environment in Japan.

In the 1960s, the economy-environment nexus, characterized by consuming an increasing amount of environmental resources with low costs, contributed to the growth regime of the high-growth era.

In the 1970s, driven by local residents' campaigns and the oil crisis, institutions for pollution abatement and energy-saving were formulated. In spite of their costs, they positively impacted growth by reducing energy importation, inducing investments, and enhancing technological competitiveness. This can be considered as an example of Green Growth.

After that, the powers of actors requesting environmental measures became weaker as damages went temporally and spatially afar. Moreover, global competition took priority over other domains of institutional coordination.

In the 1990s, public awareness and international movements led to progress in the formulation of environmental institutions, although most of them emphasized voluntariness and flexibility and did not involve a significant increase in production costs.

After 2008, institutions, such as stimulus measures aiming at Green Growth, began to be introduced under cooperation between actors on the economic and environmental sides. Stimulus measures cannot last long under budgetary constraints. Policies involving an increase in costs can form stable institutions, and would probably impact the growth positively, though the introduction of such policies depends on how the scope of cooperation between actors can be extended.

When understanding the above-mentioned evolution within the history of capitalism, after the crisis of the extensive accumulation regime in the nineteenth century, the so-called intensive accumulation regime was realized in the postwar high-growth era, though it was supported by extensive consumption of environmental resources. Today, we are facing the limits of this extensive nature of growth. Thus, the economy must be forced to change into one without extensive growth in terms of environment as well as labor, someday and somehow.

References

Boyer R (1986) La Théorie de la Régulation: Une analyse critique. La Découverte, Paris. English edition: Boyer R (1990) The regulation school: a critical introduction (trans: Charney C). Columbia University Press, New York

Central Environment Policy Council (2001) Interim report of Domestic Institutions Subcommittee, Global Environment Committee (in Japanese). http://www.env.go.jp/council/06earth/r061-01/01.pdf. Accessed 25 Nov 2016

Environment Agency (1981) Quality of the environment in Japan, 1981 (in Japanese). Environment Agency, Tokyo
Environment Agency (1991) 20-year history of the environment agency (in Japanese). Gyosei, Tokyo
Environment Agency (1992) Quality of the environment in Japan, 1992. Environment Agency, Tokyo
Environment Agency (1994) Commentary on the basic environment law (in Japanese). Gyosei, Tokyo
Kawana H (1987) Pollution in Japan: vol 1 severe pollution (in Japanese). Ryokufu, Tokyo
Kawana H (1988) Pollution in Japan: vol 2 environment agency (in Japanese). Ryokufu, Tokyo
Kawana H (1995) Pollution in Japan: vol 11 environment administrations at crossroad (in Japanese). Ryokufu, Tokyo
Ministry of the Environment, Ministry of Economy, Trade and Industry et al (2011) Policy effects of the eco-point system for green home appliances (in Japanese). http://www.env.go.jp/policy/ep_kaden/pdf/effect.pdf. Accessed 25 Nov 2016
Miyamoto K (1989) Environmental economics (in Japanese). Iwanami-shoten, Tokyo
Motani K et al (2013) Satoyama capitalism. Kadokawa, Tokyo
Murai Y (2001) Formulation and collapse of new political tribe of environment in the LDP (in Japanese). Int Polit Econ (Tsukuba University) 7:133–156
OECD (1991) Environmental performance reviews: Japan. OECD, Paris
Okuma K (2006) Characteristics and challenges of Japanese legislation for recycling of specific products: comparison with EU legislation (in Japanese). J Environ Law Policy 9:139–145
Uemura H (2000) Growth, distribution and structural change in the post-war Japanese economy. In: Boyer R, Yamada T (eds) Japanese capitalism in crisis: a régulationist interpretation. Routledge, London, pp 138–161
Uemura H (2011) Institutional changes and the transformations of the growth regime in the Japanese economy: facing the impact of the world economic crisis and Asian integration. In: Boyer R, Uemura H, Isogai A (eds) Diversity and transformations of Asian capitalisms. Routledge, London, pp 107–128
Yamada T (2008) The capitalisms: a comparative analysis (in Japanese). Fujiwara-shoten, Tokyo

Part IV
Conclusion

Chapter 10
Searching for a Vision into the Future

We have analyzed the relationship between economy and the environment theoretically as well as empirically, and have reviewed the historical evolution of this relationship. On this basis, we will now explore a vision into the future: the future of the economy and the environment, and of our society.

10.1 Where We Are Now

10.1.1 Limits of Extensive Growth and Crisis

It has been reaffirmed, through our analysis, that the economic system based on market and capital has a tendency to use labor and the environment (as the source of natural resources and the sink of wastes) in larger quantities, with lower costs, and that this needs to be controlled by institutions in order to avoid their depletion.

Looking back on the long-term history of the capitalist economy, we see that it has been growing by subsuming labor and/or the environment from the outside: in the nineteenth century, it grew extensively by acquiring labor and markets in rural communities and colonies; in the postwar golden era, it grew intensively by raising the productivity of labor while still extensively consuming the environment; after the 1970s, in spite of pollution abatements, it continued to consume large amounts of natural resources and energy (see Sect. 9.6).

Now, the scale of the economic system has exceeded the carrying capacity of the earth's ecosystem. It is impossible to continue consuming the environment as before; a major change is inevitable. The economic system needs to be controlled by strengthened environmental measures. Otherwise it must face unpredictably intensified natural disasters due to climate change, that is, a hard landing.

The economic system once overcame the crisis of the limits of extensive consumption in the labor domain by resorting to increased consumption in the

K. Okuma, *The Evolving Relationship between Economy and Environment*,
Evolutionary Economics and Social Complexity Science 8,
DOI 10.1007/978-981-10-4100-6_10

environment domain. Now we have also reached the limits there. The economic system is facing its most fundamental crisis since the establishment of capitalism.

10.1.2 Difficulties in Institutional Coordination

The socioeconomic system needs to be coordinated by institutions, in order for the economy to stop overconsuming labor and the environment. Such institutions have been formulated in the past through conflicts between stakeholders and political coordination. First, driven by labor movements, legislation and social customs protecting workers were developed. Next, driven by campaigns of residents suffering from pollution, regulatory rules for pollution abatements were formulated. But now, under the globalization of both the economy and environmental problems, institutions are not as easily formulated. The spatial and/or temporal distance between polluters and victims has become wider, disconnecting the system's feedback loop, that is, the spatial and temporal gap of coordination (see Sect. 5.1).

In the current situation, institutions in various fields, including labor, are facing pressure even for deregulation. This is because global competition has been given priority over other domains of institutions, being located in a higher position within the institutional hierarchy (see Sect. 5.2). Institutions related to labor or the environment could become stable if they were compatible with the growth regime, but otherwise they face pressure from an economy craving growth.

How can environmental institutions be formulated under such circumstances?

10.2 Green Growth and Beyond

10.2.1 Prospects for Green Growth

Looking back on history, we see a period when pollution-abatement measures contributed to growth rather than hindered it. Moreover, the analysis in this book has shown that there are now good prospects for environmental measures to contribute to growth, that is, Green Growth, by state-level policies even under the globalizing economy. Stronger environmental measures cause higher costs of production. However, in the economies of resource-importing countries with insufficient demand, it is probable that they can reduce natural resource imports by improving resource productivity, induce environmental investments in the short-term, and enhance competitiveness in environmental technologies in the mid- to long-term, all leading to a rise in demand and positively impacting economic growth. This is an environmental version of the "paradox of costs" of post-Keynesian theory, that is, the paradox of costs for environmental measures (see Sect. 5.3 and Chap. 6). Green Growth is not just a temporary stimulus. Improved economic performance in the short to midterm will enhance production capacity by improving productivity and promoting innovations, and thus can raise long-term performance.

This is good news in the current tough circumstances. In the face of heavy opposition to stricter measures, due to worries about adverse effects on growth, it can provide an immediate, realistic strategy for state-level policies to take stronger measures in such a manner as to contribute to growth through the above-mentioned positive effects.

Whether or not such a strategy is implemented is determined through coordination between stakeholders. Its results will depend not only upon how powerful new environmental actors (e.g., citizens' organizations, scientists, etc.) become, but also upon the extent to which economic and environmental actors can cooperate. Their cooperation has so far been limited to "voluntary measures" without a significant increase in production costs. The key should be whether or not the scope of cooperation can be extended to measures involving higher costs. Under the paradox of costs presented above, higher environmental costs for businesses lead to the growth of the national economy. This recognition, if widely shared, should contribute to such an extension of cooperation.

10.2.2 Need for New Approaches

However, Green Growth is not a silver bullet. The earth's ecological crisis cannot be solved by the efforts of a single state and it is not likely, or even possible, that every state aims for Green Growth. This is because the feasibility of Green Growth depends on the conditions of a given economy, for example, whether it could reduce imports of natural resources and whether it could improve technological competitiveness. Moreover, it is questionable that the world economy can continue growing forever while meeting the scientifically required conditions for ecological sustainability, for example, zero or minus emission of CO_2.

In order to overcome the structural crisis of the limits of the earth's ecosystem, the economy must be coordinated by institutions at a global scale. It must be drastically transformed so that the past trend of increasing consumption of the environment is reversed. However, we do not have a world government that can control the globally expanding economy. How can we move forward?

We recognized the driving force of institutional coordination as a feedback loop from the environment, through society, to the economy; and we have identified spatial and temporal gaps in this loop as a fundamental problem (see Sect. 5.1). Going back to this notion, we will need to search for possible mechanisms that can enhance or complement this feedback. This will require a new way of thinking beyond traditional ideas on policies.

First, a traditional recognition that policies are implemented by governments, either national or international, will need to be reconsidered. State governments are inadequate in controlling the global economy, though a world government does not exist. To begin with, policies are not neutrally designed by governmental experts, but rather are results of political coordination among relevant actors. New shapes of coordination will be generated from the thoughts and actions of various actors.

Second, a common understanding that the desirable policy can be ex ante designed should also be reconsidered. What we are facing now is not a minor amendment of the current system, but a great transformation in human history. No one clearly knows what a future sustainable society may look like. Our challenge should better be recognized as a process of searching for paths that have not yet been found.

Based on these ideas, we may be able to explore a new vision of institutional coordination and social transformation. What emerges will be a process of dynamic and pluralistic evolution, rather than a plan of static and top-down policy.

10.3 Exploring Evolutionary Economy-Environment Coordination

10.3.1 Evolution Through the Interaction of Different Levels

We try to explore, here, the possibility of such a process by considering two kinds of mechanisms. First, there should be a mechanism in which the global structure and local or individual activities evolve by interacting with each other. For example, strict international rules with tight obligations have not yet been formulated on climate change. However, an international agreement, even if not strict, is expected to generate a common understanding that stricter measures will be needed in the future, encouraging individual actors such as businesses to take actions (energy-saving, R&D, etc.). Individual actors, from their end, can strengthen the momentum to establish stricter international rules by enhancing technological developments and prospects for emission reductions. Thus, macro-level changes in global rules and micro-level changes in individual actions may interact in a positive feedback loop and coevolve.

Here, macro-level changes are not limited to the establishment of international agreements, but also include the formulation of de facto standards on environmental technologies and systems, as well as resulting economic structures where ecologically progressive companies and products gain competitive advantages and grow. As micro-level changes, not only actions by companies but also the choices of consumers and the activities of local communities can be influential. These may interact with each other and cumulatively evolve.

As regards the interaction between the macro level and the micro level, the concept of the "micro-macro loop" is important. Shiozawa (1999) called the mutually determining relationship between micro (i.e. activities of individuals) and macro (i.e. aggregated process of economy) the "micro-macro loop," intending to build a concept overcoming both methodological individualism and methodological holism. As one example, he raised the mutually supportive relationship between high economic growth and Japanese-style business management (i.e., high growth enabled the Japanese-style management style, characterized by lifetime employment and the seniority system, while that management style enabled high competitiveness through low wages and high levels of technologies). As another example, he cited the loop between buying orders by individual investors and rising stock prices in stock markets (i.e., expectations of rising stock prices encourage the buying orders of investors, while said orders raise stock prices).

The above-mentioned mechanism in environmental measures is in line with this concept of the micro-macro loop, in that it focuses on the interaction between micro individual actions and macro structures, though it is unique in that it pays particular attention to global institutions as a macro structure.[1] We may be able to call this mechanism the "micro-macro loop in environmental measures."

As one feature of the micro-macro loop of environmental measures, it should be noted that there have been some emerging activities aiming to impact the global economy. Some international environmental NGOs are running campaigns targeted to global companies, to ensure that these companies incorporate ecological considerations throughout their supply chains. This is a strategy to impact the globalizing economy beyond the territories (see Sect. 9.5). Some institutional investors are engaged in ESG investments, i.e., investments that take into consideration companies' performance in environmental, social, and governance aspects. Their main purpose is to ensure long-term profits, while the intention is also involved to make the global economy more sustainable by altering the money flow (see Sect. 9.5). These activities belong to the micro level, being behaviors of individual actors, though they consciously intend to impact the structures of the macro level. They may be recognized as mechanisms linking the micro and the macro levels.

When considering the linkage between the micro and the macro, the most important mechanism should be states. State policies impact both on individual persons/businesses and global economy/institutions. For example, the introduction of carbon taxes, tradable permits, or feed-in tariff systems in many countries is promoting the CO_2 reduction measures of businesses and renewable-energy developments in local areas, while pushing negotiations for the establishment of international rules. Strengthened country-specific regulations on automobile exhaust are promoting innovations in automobile industries (e.g., EV, hybrid, fuel cells, etc.), while influencing the international standardization of technologies. In these

[1]There are a range of views on the relationship between the micro-macro loop and institutions. Shiozawa (1999) explained that institutions exist in a special dimension, preparing stages upon which micro activities and macro aggregated processes develop, while mentioning the possibility of analyzing the relationship between institutions and actors through the framework of the micro-macro loop. Uemura et al. (2007) explained that there are double loops: one between micro actors and various institutions, and another between micro actors and macroeconomic performances. Here, while understanding that institutions can relate both to the micro and the macro, we place them in the macro in the sense that global institutions, which are our focus, are difficult for individual actors to control.

mechanisms, states can be recognized as an intermediary between the micro and the macro, rather than the final place of institutional coordination.[2]

The mechanisms described above indicate the possible coevolution of the micro and macro levels of the economy-environment nexus via their circulative interactions, enhanced by intermediating activities. This micro-macro loop of environmental measures may function as a mechanism to promote institutional coordination under the spatial and temporal gaps of coordination.

However, this should not be recognized as a mechanism that drives by itself, but rather as one that transmits the driving forces that exist somewhere under spatial or temporal gaps. This may become unstable when expectations for stricter measures change. It is not yet clear to what extent this mechanism is effective.

10.3.2 Local Experimentation

Second, we consider the potential for coordination in local areas. In local areas, economy, environment, and society are not widely separated but function in close relationship. Advanced forms of institutional coordination in the economy-environment nexus may therefore be realized in such areas, and may play an important role in the pluralistic process.

For example, there emerge various activities that try to start businesses by utilizing renewable energies or agricultural products, generating the circulation of natural resources as well as of money (see Sect. 9.5). Such activities contribute to environmental improvement and economic vitalization at the same time. They may also help restore the relationships among residents, as well as between humans and nature, possibly leading to higher well-being. Thus, they may possibly simultaneously improve the economy, environment, and society.

Viewpoints of local configurations have also been discussed in studies based on *régulation* theory (e.g., Lebougne and Lipietz 1991; Benko and Lipietz 1998; Krätke 1999). Their focus was mainly on new industrial districts in the context of transformation into post-Fordism, where the close relationships among companies, administrations, and other organizations, based on their proximity, were highlighted. Here, we consider the potential of the new local configurations in the context of transformation under the earth's ecological crisis, paying attention also to the close relationships between people and nature in local areas.

[2]On the idea of a meso level to intermediate micro and macro levels, there are a range of views, from one identifying institutions and customs as intermediates to another denying such ideas (Japan Association for Evolutionary Economics 2006). Here, recognizing the dual nature of the state, which appears as a macro system determining the conditions of activities, when viewed by individuals/companies, but appears as a micro actor, deciding and implementing policies, when seen within the global economy and international negotiations, we use the expression of "intermediate" to identify the state, focusing on its capacity to influence both the micro and the macro in certain directions.

There are some reasons for local configurations to attract attention. First, economy, environment, and society closely coexist in local areas, making institutions coordinating the economy-environment nexus easy to formulate. This is because there are no wide gaps between causes and damages, or between countermeasures and benefits, and the feedback loop from the environment to the economy works effectively. As Ostrom (1990) emphasized, the natural environment of public goods can be appropriately managed by communities in local areas. This applies basically to the coordination of local problems, and does not directly fill the spatial and temporal gap of coordination for global environmental problems. However, measures for local problems often have positive effects on global problems. For example, appropriate forest management contributes not only to better landscapes and disaster management in local areas, but also to maintaining biodiversity and absorbing CO_2.

Second, there are relatively rich natural resources in local areas, through the use of which new value can be generated. Examples include renewable energies such as biomass or wind power; agricultural products with higher added values, such as organic brands; and tourist businesses such as eco-tourism. Through activities that simultaneously reduce environmental burdens and create new value, institutional coordination that is compatible with the growth regime of the regional economy may be realized.

Third, concentrated activities in local areas may generate innovations in the economy-environment nexus. Innovations include not only technological ones but also social ones such as institutions or systems. The role of regional human and organizational networks in generating innovations was emphasized by the Californian School of Economic Geography (e.g., Storper 1997; Scott 1998) and made well known through the concept of clusters by Porter (1998). These studies focus on external economies generated from networks of companies, universities, and other organizations. Here, networks of natural and human resources in a region may generate technological and social innovations on the economy-environment nexus. Moreover, induced innovations spread into other regions via competition and imitation. Such phenomena occur in reality: advanced regions of renewable energy development have emerged, offering models for other regions: for example, Freiburg in Germany, Samso Island in Denmark, and Gussing in Austria.

Thus, in local areas where economy, environment, and society closely coexist, new models of socioeconomic configuration can be explored, which may also lead to a future transformation of the whole society. Such an idea exists in the domain where ecological economics and evolutionary economics overlap. In ecological economics, Norgaard (1994) proposed a vision of coevolution of ecosystem and social system in the "patchwork quilt" of cultures around the globe. Recognizing that modernization, assuming progress by a single model of technology and social organization, has "betrayed" us, as is apparent in the sustainability crisis, he suggested that different forms of development be explored by regionally diverse societies.

This vision can be theoretically elaborated by evolutionary economics. Ellerman (2014) presented the concept of "parallel experimentation" in the process of evolution. He focused on the importance of parallel experiments, in addition to series experiments; this was illustrated as the importance of "jumping to the other hills" instead of climbing one hill when it is found to be low. Referring to a process seen in biological evolution—in which the drifting of genes is promoted by subdividing the population into small subgroups whose successful genes are then selected and defused to other groups—he pointed out that parallel experiments by small groups are also important in the process of economic evolution, especially under uncertainties.

In search of new modes of *régulation* under the crisis of environmental constraints, parallel experimentation should play an essential role. Experiments in this context can be conducted in a variety of units, such as states, companies, regions, etc. Among these, local experiments under close relationship with natural capital should be of special importance.

Looking back, the world socioeconomic system appears to be proceeding in the direction of integration and homogenization under the globalizing economy.[3] This system as a whole is entering into crisis as it faces the limits of the earth's ecosystem. If it is a crisis of one region among multiple regions, or of one system among multiple systems, then the whole can continue to develop by selecting better ones under the evolutionary process, just as animals and plants have continuously evolved even when some populations fail. However, if the world economy becomes one integrated system and it crashes in the crisis, then modern civilization may fail as a whole.

On the other hand, if diverse forms of socioeconomic configuration are prepared through local experiments, then, in the face of changing conditions, forms better fitting them can be chosen and diffused. Thus, advanced and diverse models developed in local areas can possibly work as footholds to overcome the great transformation into the future. They can act as "beachheads toward the future," so to speak.

However, the economic system is expanding by subsuming other territories. Under this mechanism, it will not be easy to maintain and develop unique forms of coordination in local areas.[4] How can conditions that enable diverse configurations be ensured? This should be an issue to be further considered.

10.3.3 Changing but Still Important Roles of States

These are rough descriptions of the possible evolutionary mechanisms. We need to search for such new mechanisms. This will require efforts, including trial and error, at every level of actor.

---

[3]As VOC theory (Hall and Soskice 2001) and *régulation* theory (Amable 2003) emphasize, the capitalist economies of states are not homogeneous but diverse. However, as international competition becomes superior, room for diverse coordination by states appears to be getting smaller.

[4]When new industrial districts attracted attention as regional structures of post-Fordism, they already raised concerns that local institutional coordination would not be easy to maintain under a global neoliberal economy (Peck and Tickell 1994).

In this process, the roles of states must be important. Under the globalizing economy facing the crisis of the earth's ecosystem, states can no longer be the final authority for institutional coordination. However, designing and implementing advanced institutions at the state level will be an important driving force in the coevolutionary process of the micro and the macro described above.

For example, states can set standards and price incentives for products, as well as giving support to local developments in the search for sustainable regions. They can thus encourage innovations in business activities and regional policies. This can be a strategy under dynamic competition, meaning a state policy that is compatible with the competitive international regime. Moreover, states can share their experiences to disseminate such policies, and further advocate making them global standards or rules.

So far, varieties of new policy schemes have been introduced by states. Many of them were first invented by environmentally advanced states, then followed by many other countries learning from their experiences, and have now become global de facto standards of policies. Experiments by each state can generate worldwide evolution of policies.

States can not only act individually, but can also implement common policies and thus jointly lead the formulation of global institutions. In particular, regional integration mechanisms such as the EU can also play important roles in the evolution of environmental policies.

The role of the states, here, has been changed from that of the past: it is taking on the character of an intermediating mechanism between global institutional coordination and local or individual activities, rather than being seen as the final authority of institutional coordination. In spite of this change, its importance is still enormous.

Green Growth should be an effective way for states to play this role. By pursuing Green Growth, they will be able to strengthen environmental measures with wider political support. Using the time and resources that this buys, they should then implement policies with a longer-range perspective aiming at dynamic and evolutionary effects. Thus, they may be able to prepare for more fundamental changes, in addition to achieving short- to midterm improvements.

10.4 Challenges Ahead of Us

10.4.1 Social Globalization and Economy Without External Expansion

We have just explored some mechanisms for a possible evolutionary process. Where will they bring us?

These mechanisms may, to some extent, bridge the gaps between the global economy and its governance, but they will not work automatically. Mechanisms need their driving forces. As history shows, institutions will not be formulated without the power of actors calling for them. For global environmental problems, the damages from which occur in future generations or remote places, someone needs to transmit or represent the voices of those affected. This will probably require civil societies that extend their recognition and sympathy beyond time and space and take action. This may be called social globalization, in response to the globalizing economy.

This is not an easy task. The good news is that the forecasts of damages and information-sharing have been significantly improved, thanks to science and information technologies. However, recent political developments in the world indicate that nationalism is getting stronger. Even after the damages of climate change have become evident, nation-states could pursue national adaptive measures (e.g., disaster management) while neglecting global and essential countermeasures, even though the science warns us that climate change will be too harsh to adapt to, if not mitigated by emission reductions.

Can social globalization, that is, the extension of recognition and the sympathy beyond time and place, be realized at all? Will it gradually progress, once the damages become evident and the sense of crisis is shared beyond borders? Can it be achieved in time to avoid catastrophic changes in the global environment?

When thinking about economic growth, Green Growth can be a realistic strategy for the moment, which can be taken on by individual states. However, it is not likely that the economy can grow forever while significantly reducing environmental burdens.[5] Looking back on the history of the capitalist economy, it has never realized growth without external expansion in labor or the environment. Moreover, the world economy appears to be exploring frontiers from emerging economies to less developed countries, thus assuming a still stronger character of extensive accumulation. The real issue is the fundamental change of these trends (see Sect. 9.6).

To begin with, economic growth and human welfare are different concepts. What we should really aim at is not to increase GDP, as measured by money, but to enable people to live happier and more meaningful lives. Now that we have become materially rich (though the materials are not equitably distributed), what we really want will be connection with nature, involvement in culture and art, knowledge toward the truth, freedom to live as desired, and other longings that vary from

[5]There are views that structural changes toward economies centering on information and services would enable continuous growth. This may be regarded as a transformation to the society emphasizing intellectual/spiritual values than material ones. However, it should not be neglected that information always involves matter and energy as media, as Daly (1996) pointed to. Moreover, it should be questioned whether wider market-transaction of knowledge and information is really desirable or not, because enclosing them for trade out of freely shared commons may impede intellectual or spiritual development of the whole society. As the emerging hypothesis of "cognitive capitalism" indicates, it may have a hidden meaning that the extensive expansion of the production system finally reaches the domain of knowledge and life beyond labor and the environmental resources (e.g. Moulier-Boutang 2011).

person to person but that are commonly spiritual rather than material.[6] Qualitative development, rather than quantitative growth, would be the real goal.

Even so, the system of the capitalist economy is driven by the quest for profit, requiring growth. When growth could not be realized, the socioeconomic system has struggled under the crisis, resorting to block economies and even fascism in the 1930s. This past history does not allow us to easily hold optimistic visions for the future.

When there is no room for external expansion, in the face of the limits of the earth's ecosystem, will it be possible for the economy to continue growing only by improving productivity? When this becomes difficult and the only possibility becomes very low or even minus growth, can the economic system endure it? There may be scrambles for environmental resources, in the search for growth, causing international conflicts. Will the world be able to equitably share the natural environment?

Humankind is now facing an unprecedented challenge to maintain the capitalist economy without externally expanding it.

10.4.2 Toward the Second Great Transformation

The world economy, facing the crisis in the first half of the twentieth century, transformed from a free-market economy to one coordinated by welfare states. Polanyi (1957) called this "the great transformation." Then, as the free-market economy has resurged with prevailing global competition since the end of the twentieth century, the possibility of "the second great transformation" has been mentioned at times (e.g. Boyer 1992). The world economy will sooner or later be forced to change significantly, facing the crisis of the earth's ecosystem. This change from the environmental aspect should be the largest factor of the second great transformation.

This great transformation will not be something that is designed in advance, but that is formulated through political coordination among various stakeholders, as was the case in the first great transformation. Moreover, as with that transformation, which involved such a deep agony that two world wars occurred, the second great transformation will also involve considerable, possibly even worse, difficulties.

Even so, it holds significant meaning, in this process, to search for future visions and to advance toward them as individuals or organizations. Ilya Prigogine revealed that, in a complex system of a chaotic state, a new order of the system may be generated from small fluctuations (Prigogine and Stengers 1984). Individual recognitions and actions may possibly have impacts on the direction of the whole society, under severe crises and structural changes.

[6] Sen (1999) emphasized the importance of freedom to live a life that one has reason to value and of capability to enable it as the aim of economic development.

We are now facing an unprecedented challenge to make decisions as a society, beyond the spatial borders of states and temporal borders of generations, and to coordinate the market economy by institutions.

Looking back, modern civilization has left the task of coordinating the socio-economic system to the "money" of the market mechanism. By doing so, perhaps we have been saving ourselves the effort of formulating institutions.

In the process of tackling this challenge, we will be required to recognize the world more deeply and sympathize with others more widely. Moreover, each of us will need to take individual actions, searching for a new shape of world. This will mean more fully exerting our human abilities.

Economy and the environment evolve, and so does the world. Humans are also required to change. What will be waiting for us beyond this challenge?

References

Amable B (2003) The diversity of modern capitalism. Oxford University Press, Oxford

Benko G, Lipietz A (1998) From the regulation of space to the space of regulation. GeoJournal 44 (4):275–281

Boyer R (1992) The second grand transformation (in Japanese; trans: Inoue Y). Fujiwara-shoten, Tokyo

Daly H (1996) Beyond growth: the economics of sustainable development. Beacon Press, Boston

Ellerman D (2014) Parallel experimentation: a basic sheme for dynamic efficiency. J Bioecon 16:259–287

Hall P, Soskice D (eds) (2001) Varieties of capitalism: the institutional foundations of comparative advantage. Oxford University Press, Oxford

Japan Association for Evolutionary Economics (2006) Handbook of evolutionary economics (in Japanese). Kyouritsu, Tokyo

Krätke S (1999) A regulationist approach to regional studies. Environ Plan A 31:687–704

Lebougne D, Lipietz A (1991) Two social strategies in the production of new industrial spaces. In: Benko G, Dunford M (eds) Industrial change and regional development: the transformation of new industrial spaces. Belhaven Press, London, pp 27–50

Moulier-Boutang Y (2011) Cognitive capitalism. Polity, Cambridge

Norgaard RB (1994) Development betrayed: the end of progress and a coevolutionary revisioning of the future. Routledge, New York

Ostrom E (1990) Governing the commons: the evolution of institutions for collective action. Cambridge University Press, Cambridge

Peck J, Tickell A (1994) Searching for a new institutional fix: the after-Fordist crisis and the global-local disorder. In: Amin A (ed) Post-Fordism: a reader. Blackwell, Oxford, pp 280–315

Polanyi K (1957) Great transformation. Beacon Press, Boston

Porter ME (1998) On competition. Harvard Business School Press, Boston

Prigogine I, Stengers I (1984) Order out of chaos: mans' new dialogue with nature. Alvin Toffler Bantam Books, New York

Scott AJ (1998) Regions and the world economy: the coming shape of global production, competition, and political order. Oxford University Press, Oxford

Sen A (1999) Development as freedom. Alfred A Knopf, New York

Shiozawa Y (1999) On micro-macro loop (in Japanese). Keizai Ronsou (Kyoto University) 164 (5):1–73

Storper M (1997) The regional world: territorial development in a global economy. Guilford Press, New York

Uemura H, Isogai A, Ebizuka A (2007) Institutional analysis of socioeconomic system (in Japanese). The University of Nagoya Press, Nagoya

Appendix: Data Sources and Estimation Methods

Emission of Carbon Dioxide
Value of the National Greenhouse Gas Inventory Report of JAPAN (National Institute for Environmental Studies 2012) is used from 1990 on. Value estimated by Oak Ridge Laboratory (Borden et al. 2014), connected to the above, is used before that.

Emission of Sulfur Oxides
Value in Japan's Third National Communication under the United Nations Framework Convention on Climate Change (UNFCCC) is used for the 1990s. Value in Japan Research Institute (1998) (originally estimated by the National Institute of Science and Technology Policy) is used for every 5 years from 1970 to 1990. Value estimated by Li and Dai (2000) is used before 1970. For other years, we estimated emission by using the General Survey of the Emission of Air Pollutants (in Japanese) by the Ministry of the Environment.

Internal Pollution Control Cost
Following the method in Japan Research Institute (2004), we estimated the maintenance cost of the pollution-abatement plants and equipment based on the accumulated value of investment. (Concretely, the acquisition value of existing plants and equipment is estimated as investment accumulated for 20 years, and the maintenance cost is estimated as 10% of it.) The investment was estimated by combining the ratio of investment for pollution-abatement purpose to total investment (or equivalent ratio for some periods) in Survey of Plants and Equipment Investment (in Japanese) by Ministry of Economy, Trade, and Industry (METI) and the value of investment in Japan Industrial Productivity (JIP) Database by Research Institute of Economy, Trade, and Industry. Data from METI's Survey of Pollution Abatement Investment (in Japanese) were also used for the earlier periods for which the above-mentioned data was not available.

K. Okuma, *The Evolving Relationship between Economy and Environment*,
Evolutionary Economics and Social Complexity Science 8,
DOI 10.1007/978-981-10-4100-6

Internal Energy-Saving Cost

Following the same method as above, we estimated the maintenance cost of the energy-saving plants and equipment based on the accumulated value of investment. The investment was estimated by combining the ratio of investment for energy-saving purpose to total investment (or equivalent ratio for some periods) in METI's Survey of Plants and Equipment Investment (in Japanese) and the value of investment in JIP Database. Data from Survey on Planned Capital Spending (in Japanese) by the Development Bank of Japan were also used for the earlier periods for which the above-mentioned data was not available.

Waste Management Cost

Value of intermediate input from the waste management sector to other sectors in JIP Database is used. Extension in the trend of pollution control cost and linear interpolation were also conducted for the earlier periods for which the above-mentioned data was not available.

Environmental Research and Development

Internal research expenditure for the purpose of environmental protection in Survey of Research and Development by the Ministry of Internal Affairs and Communications is used.

Import of Natural Resources

Values of import of particular items in Trade Statistics of Japan by the Ministry of Finance are used.

Maintenance Cost of SO_x and NO_x

Following the method in Japan Research Institute (1998), we estimated the maintenance cost by multiplying emissions of SO_x and NO_x from fixed sources, and their unit reduction costs. As for unit reduction costs, values in 1995 were consistently used. Emission of NO_x from fixed sources is estimated by the same method as sulfur oxides except for using data in Li and Dai (2000).

Maintenance Cost of CO_2

Following the method in Japan Research Institute (1998), we estimated the maintenance cost by multiplying excessive emission calculated as emission minus nature's absorption, and unit reduction cost. As for unit reduction cost, one for 6% reduction from 1990 were consistently used.

Accumulation Rate

Value of "private sectors" in "gross fixed capital formation" in the System of National Accounts (SNA) divided by capital stock is used.

Profit Rate

Profit (explained below), divided by capital stock (explained below), is used.

Capital Stock

Data in Gross Capital Stock of Private Sectors by Cabinet Office is used.

Wage and Profit

Following the method in Yoshikawa (1994) with referring to Uni (1998), we estimated wage and net profit in private sectors by estimating distribution ratio between wage and net profit in corporations and assuming this ratio applies to private unincorporated entities. Then, we estimated gross profit by adding consumption of fixed capital in private sectors to net profit. It should be noted that we added interest when calculating profit of total private sectors instead of doing so when estimating distribution rate in corporations under the recognition that interest includes profit of both corporations and unincorporated entities. Concretely, they are estimated by the following equations:

$$\text{(Wage in private corporations)} = \text{[Compensation of employee]} - \text{(Adjustment factor)[Entrepreneurial income in private unincorporated entities]} - \text{[Employment income in public offices]}$$

$$\text{(Net profit in private corporations)} = \text{[Entrepreneurial income of private corporations]} + \text{[Dividends in household property income]}$$

$$\text{(Wage in private unincorporated entities)} = \text{[Entrepreneurial income of private unincorporated entities]}\{1 + \text{(Adjustment factor)}\}\text{(Distribution ratio to wage in private corporations)}$$

$$\text{(Net profit in private unincorporated entities)} = \text{[Entrepreneurial income of private unincorporated entities]}\{1 + \text{(Adjustment factor)}\}\text{(Distribution ratio to net profit in private corporations)}$$

$$\text{(Wage)} = \text{(Wage in private corporations)} + \text{(Wage in private unincorporated entities)}$$

$$\text{(Gross profit)} = \text{(Net profit in private corporations)} + \text{(Net profit in private unincorporated entities)} + \text{[Interest in household property income]} + \text{[Consumption of fixed capital in private sectors]}$$

where members in square brackets are data from SNA except for [Employment income in public office] from National Tax Agency Annual Statistics Report; (adjustment factor) is the ratio of salaries and wages to net operating profit in Unincorporated Enterprise Survey.

Output

We calculated output, in the definition of this book, by adding import to the sum of wage and gross profit estimated above.

Saving

We estimated gross saving by adding consumption of fixed capital to saving in SNA.

Capacity Utilization Rate
We estimated capacity utilization rate of private sectors, excluding governmental sectors, by using the capital utilizing index in the JIP Database. We made an extension in the trend of operating ratio in Indices of Industrial Production by METI for the earlier periods for which the above-mentioned data was not available.

Production Capital, Wage for Production Labor, Profit for Production Capital, and Rent for Production Resources
We first estimated capital stock for environmental measures from investments for pollution control and energy saving estimated in "Internal Pollution Control Cost" and "Internal Energy-saving Cost" above (depreciation of fixed rate of 7% was assumed), and then estimated production capital by subtracting it from capital stock. We estimated wage for production labor by multiplying wage by the value of 1 minus the ratio of environmental-measure costs to output. The same applies to profit for production capital and rent for production resources. These values were used in calculating ratio of output to production capital, share of wage for production labor, share of profit for production capital, and share of rent for production resources.

Accumulated Experiences in Environmental Measures
We calculated the amount of environmental measures represented in their costs (on real basis) as accumulated per the function ($T_t = E_t + (1 - \delta)T_{t-1}$) shown in Chap. 6, assuming depreciation rate of technological knowledge (δ) as 10%.

References

Borden TA, Marland G, Andres RJ (2014) Regional and national fossil-fuel CO_2 emissions. Carbon Dioxide Information Analysis Center, Oak Ridge National Laboratory, US Department of Energy, Oak Ridge, Tenn. doi 10.3334/CDIAC/00001_V2013

Japan Research Institute (1998) Report on estimation of the integrated environmental and economic accounting (in Japanese). Japan Research Institute, Tokyo

Japan Research Institute (2004) Report on reconstruction of the integrated environmental and economic accounting after the revision of SEEA (in Japanese). Japan Research Institute, Tokyo

Li ZD, Dai YD (2000) Japan-China comparative analysis on measures against sulfur oxides pollution (in Japanese). Energy Economics 26(3):2–20, Institute of Energy Economics, Tokyo

National Institute for Environmental Studies (2012) National greenhouse gas inventory report of Japan. http://www-gio.nies.go.jp/aboutghg/nir/nir-updated_nir_j.html. Accessed 24 Nov 2016

Uni H (1998) Structural change and capital accumulation (in Japanse). Yuhikaku, Tokyo

Yoshikawa H (1994) Distribution ratio to labor and growth/circulation of Japanese economy (in Japanese). In: Ishikawa T (ed) Distribution of income and wealth in Japan (in Japanese). University of Tokyo Press, Tokyo, pp 107–140

The manufacturer's authorised representative in the EU is Springer Nature Customer Service Centre GmbH, Europaplatz 3, 69115 Heidelberg, Germany. If you have any concerns regarding our products, please contact ProductSafety@springernature.com

Printed and bound by CPI Group (UK) Ltd, Croydon, CR0 4YY
25/09/2026
02222806-0010